CROSSING OVER

CROSSING OVER

LIBERATING THE
TRANSGENDERED
CHRISTIAN

VANESSA SHERIDAN

THE
PILGRIM
PRESS
Cleveland

For my transgendered sisters and brothers
engaged in the struggle for spiritual liberation

The Pilgrim Press, 700 Prospect Avenue E.,
Cleveland, Ohio 44115-1100, U.S.A.
pilgrimpress.com

Printed in the United States of America on acid-free paper

Library of Congress Cataloging-in-Publication Data
Sheridan, Vanessa, 1949-
    Crossing over : liberating the transgendered Christian / Vanessa
Sheridan.
      p. cm.
    ISBN 0-8298-1446-9
    1. Transsexualism – Religious aspects – Christianity. 2. Christian
transsexuals – Religious life. I. Title.
BR115.T76 S47 2001
261.8′3576 – dc21

2001036061

CONTENTS

FOREWORD

MARK TWAIN once observed that there are two kinds of people in the world: people who divide people into two kinds of people, and people who don't. Many of us aspire to be counted with Twain's latter group. We want to be inclusive. We want to celebrate human diversity. We realize that any bifurcation of reality into two kinds is a falsification.

Nevertheless, when it comes to the sex of human beings, many of us still divide people into two obviously different kinds: female and male. Thus, it was no surprise to hear a liberal pastor friend's comment recently. Regarding gay, lesbian, bisexual, and transgendered persons, he remarked that he thought he did well with the G's, the L's, and the B's—but the T's were really hard for him.

He is not alone. For years I made a clear distinction between sex and gender. Sex, I assumed, was our biology. It was, at least for the vast majority of human beings, the unambiguous maleness or femaleness with which we were born. Our genitals were the clue, and one look by the attending doctor, nurse, or midwife was enough for the definitive message, "It's a girl," or, "It's a boy." Only in a tiny fraction of instances was there genital ambiguity. On the other hand, *gender*—the *meanings* of our biological sex, our masculinity and femininity—was always socially constructed and learned. Those were my assumptions.

In more recent years I have come to appreciate how important social construction is not only to our genders but also to our sex itself, our maleness and femaleness. Readers will find Vanessa Sheridan's book extraordinarily helpful in understanding how this is so. Describing her own experience and that of other transgendered persons she knows, she gives us sensitive, honest portrayals and insightful interpretations—dramatically different from the typical sensationalism we encounter in media accounts. She dispels the ignorance and false myths that have fed fears of the transgendered and gives us an excellent analysis of transgenderphobia. In all of this, she speaks compellingly from inside the experience, not as a dispassionate observer.

Beyond examination of the psychodynamics of anti-transgender bias, Vanessa Sheridan invites us into theological reflection. Well-grounded in liberation theology, she presents the reader with suggestive possibilities of the transgendered church and the transgendered dimensions of Christ and God. Such reflection is not only evocative but also, I hope, a prelude to additional and exciting theological work awaiting us in the future.

But why should the majority in the religious community, we who are not transgendered, care about these issues? I want to underscore and elaborate on several arguments I see in this persuasive book.

—We should care because it is a matter of elemental justice and human dignity for these persons who are God's beloved creatures. The higher-than-average instances of depression, anxiety disorders, familial alienation, chemical abuse, depression, and suicide are the results of social oppression—experiences common to virtually every oppressed group. Caring is a matter of simple justice mandated by prophetic faith.

—We should care because it is a gender-liberating matter. One of the important gifts transgendered people offer is the possibility of greater gender liberation for all the rest of us. And, I would add, particularly for men. For a host of reasons, men have more trouble with these matters. Masculinity is a hard-earned, never-finished, always insecure identity in this society, and the transgendered can be threatening to those who have anxieties about their own manhood. Further, men tend to be more alienated from their bodies, and body-alienation has a predictable corollary: resistance to ambiguity and rigid insistence on either/or's. And, in a sexist society, men have a vested interest in maintaining the ancient sexual dualism of spirit vs. body and men over women: it preserves men's power. The difficulties in men's liberation are great, but the promises are enormous, both personally and socially.

—We should care because it is a matter of the soul of the church. To be true to the Gospel, the church must always live in a creative, transforming tension with culture. The fact of the matter is that, by and large, our culture is not only transgenderphobic, but also "genderist." Phobias describe the emotional dynamics of persons; the "isms" describe what is built into institutions. Not only are irrational fears about transgendered persons prevalent, but also anti-transgender bias is firmly institutionalized and enforced by clear social sanctions. Historically, the church has always endangered its soul when it has capitulated uncritically to its surrounding culture. The inclusion of, affirmation of, and celebration of transgendered people within the church is truly counterculture.

In a day when many of us in the "mainline" denominations are beginning to realize that we are no longer religiously at the center of our culture, the invitation to reconsider our counterculture vocation can be lifesaving. Marginalization is not merely a threat; it can also be a gift. Transgendered people know what it is like to live on the margins of society. They have much to teach the rest of the church.

Most church judicatories and congregations have consciously struggled for several decades now with issues of sexual orientation. Gay men, lesbians, and bisexuals are being heard more frequently and in some parts of the church are finding certain forms of affirmation. However, issues of sexual identity posed by crossdressing, transsexual, and intersexual people are much newer for the churches and, I believe, even more difficult. After all, the female-male distinction is perhaps the earliest and most basic way most of us begin to sort out the world. When the clarity and simplicity of that is challenged, our perceptual worlds can be shaken.

But there is so much to be gained for everyone. So we who are not transgendered must listen—listen hard—to transgendered voices, of which Vanessa Sheridan's is particularly thoughtful and theologically challenging.

Why must we listen hard? Again, it is a matter of simple justice. Truly listening to anyone invariably communicates a sense of worth and dignity that the other deserves.

We also must listen remembering Dietrich Bonhoeffer's warning written from an underground seminary: "Many people are looking for an ear that will listen. They do not find it among Christians, because these Christians are talking where they should be listening. But [the one] who can no longer listen to . . . brother [or sister] will soon be not listening to God either. . . . This is the beginning of the death of the spiritual life, and in the end there is nothing left."[1]

In addition, we must listen to our transgendered sisters and brothers because, as liberation theology reminds us, we who have dominant power simply do not hear or see many holy things. But the oppressed have keen ears and wide eyes. For example, they often see more clearly where God is at work bringing down the powerful from their thrones, lifting up the lowly, filling the hungry with good things, and sending the rich away empty (Luke 1:51–52).

So I am exceedingly grateful to Vanessa Sheridan for her articulate witness. She knows well that there are more than two kinds of people. She also knows well that in spite of the important differences in the varieties of sexual identities we bear, there is finally only one kind of people: God's people.

Knowing that, she and many other transgendered people have chosen to stay with the church. They have had many reasons to vote with their feet, but they have stayed because they believe that the Gospel is for everyone, not just for some. They have stayed, believing that the church might yet be a bigger church. Bigger in its integrity. Larger in its ability to stand in connection with all marginalized people. Bigger in its strength of spirit to enable all of us to realize our destiny to freedom, uniqueness, and worth. Yes, a church larger in the size of its soul.

JAMES B. NELSON
Professor Emeritus of Christian Ethics
United Theological Seminary of the Twin Cities

PREFACE

There are more things in
Heaven and earth, Horatio,
Than are dreamt of in your philosophy.
            —*Hamlet,* I, v, 16

HOW CAN THE INSTITUTIONAL CHURCH exist or operate
with integrity if it unjustly shuns, rejects, marginal-
izes, or oppresses some human beings based upon the
arbitrary criteria of gender orientation or gender presentation? Responses to that question are critical if the church
is to genuinely be the Body of Christ for the world and for
all of its citizens. In this book I explore those responses,
encourage Christians to embrace transgendered people into
the full life and ministry of the church, and consider ways
in which differently gendered persons can experience and
work for liberation through the church.

By asking questions like this, I do not mean to under-
mine or dismiss the church as an irrelevant or unnecessary
institution. The Christian church is my spiritual heritage,
and I love it with all my heart. However, loving the church
means that I cannot always support its actions, behaviors,
or attitudes, especially when they harm or exclude others;
looking at the church with a constructively critical eye is
essential. Catholic monk Thomas Merton, in *He Is Risen,*
reminds us,

> The Christian must have the courage to follow Christ.
> The Christian who is risen in Christ must dare to be
> like Christ: he [*sic*] must dare to follow conscience even
> in unpopular causes. He must, if necessary, be able to

disagree with the majority and make decisions that he knows to be according to the Gospel and teaching of Christ, even when others do not understand why he is acting this way.[1]

Jesus was an outsider and a rebel, at least in the view of the religious and social establishment of his day. He was different: an unconventional risk-taker, a dreamer, a trailblazer, a pioneer, a prophet of change, a social and religious radical, a person who managed to anger almost everyone, and one who placed love of God and of God's creation above everything else, including the false, unjust teachings of humanly devised religion. If we are to call ourselves Christians—"little Christs," followers of Jesus—then we must, in good conscience, also attempt to emulate Jesus and be "different."

Being different in the context of the Christian church is not always easy, however. The pressure toward religious homogeneity is strong and insistent; those who go against the grain do not usually have a smooth path or a comfortable pilgrimage. We who are different are also the ones who ostensibly threaten the status quo, a condition that our institutions are passionately devoted to protecting. Yet, as Robert Frost told us, it's often the road less traveled by that makes all the difference. Those less-traveled roads can make an extraordinarily interesting and fulfilling journey.

As I continue on my personal journey of faith, I have been interested in and influenced by the theological implications of my transgendered status for a number of years and have become increasingly aware of the significance of those implications for my life and for the lives of others. I find my commitment growing toward working to create a more generalized public awareness of the lives of transgendered persons, particularly from a theological perspective. I'm convinced that this is important, not necessarily because I'm doing it but because the lives of my differently gendered sisters and brothers *matter*.

Along the way, I have observed that some (certainly not all, but some) evangelicals, religious conservatives, and biblical literalists appear to present a rather unattractive legalistic and spiritually arrogant demeanor toward those who differ or disagree with their particular interpretation of scripture. These symptoms may simply be representative of religious indigestion, a condition frequently caused by swallowing the spiritually and intellectually unhealthy tenets of biblical literalism. Harvard theology professor Peter J. Gomes informs us that adherents of a biblical literalist interpretive approach tend to comprise "a cadre of cultural conservatives [who] would rather defend their ideology in the name of the authority of scripture than concede that their self-serving reading of that scripture just might be wrong, and that both the Bible and the God who inspires it may be more gracious, just, and inclusive than they can presently afford to be."[2] I pray that God's accepting, inclusive love might become increasingly present in the lives of such persons. The world needs more compassion and humility, not more spiritual self-importance or religious conceit. We need people who care more about following the example of Jesus, doing the work of justice, and serving the living God than they do about idolatrously and dogmatically falling at the feet of a literalist interpretive tradition.

I also find myself spiritually compelled to strive for the legitimate transformation of the church into a more responsive and responsible entity, one that truly enacts and embodies the love of God for all humankind. As long as the institutional church remains mired in its patriarchal, androcentric, hierarchical, and sex/gender-phobic paradigms, it will be greatly diminished in its capacity to act effectively and compassionately toward all people on our Creator's behalf. This is precisely why a transformation of the church is absolutely essential and why thinking Christians need to work unceasingly for positive change within our beloved but ailing institution. It's also why we must, in good conscience, struggle against the many institutional gods (with a small "g") that are actively arrayed against us: the gods of apathy, of greed, of ignorance, and of exploitative power wielded against the disenfranchised and powerless.

Transforming the entrenched institution of the church will not be easy, and we shouldn't expect it to be. The hard work of transformation will be confusing at times, incredibly frustrating, almost always difficult, and fraught with dangers and potential pitfalls. This is a perilous, tough, challenging task, to be sure. Yet, it is necessary for Christians to actively commit ourselves to and involve ourselves in this transformative effort because the souls of human beings are at stake. God's accepting, inclusive love must be shared with the world, no matter the cost.

As we proceed it is critical for us to remember that Christian orthodoxy is not necessarily orthodox because it is right, but simply because it happened to win out over other theological points of view at a certain time in history.[3] The church that I love so much has, unfortunately, tended to encourage spiritual dependency while frequently seeking to direct and restrain rather than enhance and empower the lives of its members. It is time to increase our awareness of that unhappy situation and then to do something about it.

This book is intended to provide useful information and to serve as a resource on transgendered Christian spiritual experience for laypersons as well as clergy, pastoral counselors, and other church leaders. I have attempted to present this information so others might better understand the scope and varied dynamics of transgendered Christianity as well as other closely related personal and social issues affecting the gender variant Christian.

Writers and their readers share a special, highly personalized relationship. Each individual brings unique qualities and perspectives to that fragile but potentially life-changing writer/reader association. As you read through these pages it is my hope that you and I may somehow forge our own distinctive connection, one grounded in mutual respect,

honesty, and integrity. In doing so we will surely reap many
benefits as together we explore the intricacies and begin the
construction of a transgender theology of liberation.

"Some say that the very purpose of human existence is
to get acquainted with your own essential qualities and express them in your daily activities. Whether it is the purpose
of life or not, it is a fine definition of personal creativity:
living every moment from your Essence."[4] I am humbly
striving toward that worthy goal of acquaintance, expression, and living every moment from my God-given Essence.
This work is the collective result of many influences and
experiences, and I am deeply grateful to all those who have
taught me or shared those experiences with me.

To the best of my knowledge, this is the first book by a
transgendered author on the topic of transgender Christian
spirituality ever to be published by a mainstream publishing house; I trust it will not be the last. I am extremely
pleased and humbled to be associated with a publishing
organization with such pioneering foresight and courage.
These issues are pretty revolutionary for some. Nevertheless, they are issues whose time has come, and The Pilgrim
Press has risen boldly to the challenge. I am especially indebted to my editor, George R. Graham, for his help, for
his insights and enthusiasm, and for believing.

I want to thank my friends who have encouraged me
to learn, to grow, to increase my awareness, to write, and
to continue "becoming." The staff, faculty, and students at
United Theological Seminary of the Twin Cities have been
inspirational for me in more ways than I can enumerate.
I am also profoundly grateful to many of my sisters and
brothers in the local and national transgender community.
They are gifted, unique, diverse, and interesting; they make
me proud to call myself transgendered.

I owe a deep debt of gratitude to my friends Jim Nelson,
Patrick Gambill-Read, and Jade Devlin for their contributions to this book. They are extraordinary human beings,
and God continues to do important work through them.

Many thanks, as well, to the transgendered individuals who have shared their stories in these pages.

I thank God every day for the unwavering support of my extraordinary spouse; we have been through much together, and I continue to learn and benefit from her example of Christlike love. I have no idea what she sees in me, but she seems determined to love me despite my obvious eccentricities and idiosyncrasies. I am also blessed to have a wonderful family; they are beautiful, incredible, and precious to me. And last, but certainly not least, I am forever grateful to my Creator, Redeemer, and Sustainer for the myriad of blessings that have been so richly bestowed upon my life. I am painfully aware of my own flaws and shortcomings, but I also know that I am loved with a profoundly mysterious, unfathomable, and eternal divine love, a love that totally defies my extremely finite powers of comprehension and articulation. God is amazingly good.

1

ON BEING DIFFERENT

I T WAS A HOT, sticky Sunday morning in central Florida, and the thirteen-year-old boy was sitting in one of the back pews of his Southern Baptist church with a few of his friends. They always sat in the back on Sunday mornings. It was easier to whisper and pass notes during the sermon, and from that vantage point they could more readily avoid detection by parents and the hellfire-and-brimstone preacher.

The boy had been brought up in a fundamentalist Southern Baptist home and had been instructed throughout his childhood that the Bible was the inspired, infallible, inerrant Word of God. The literal words of scripture were never to be questioned or interpreted in any manner other than the one his evangelical-conservative church espoused. The belief system into which he had been thoroughly indoctrinated required only unreflective and unquestioning obedience to the legalistic teachings of his denomination. Besides, he was really a good boy—rather sensitive, in fact—and he didn't want to cause problems for anyone. He loved his family, he loved his church, and he wanted to love God, but, to be truthful, in his heart of hearts he was afraid of God. God, he was convinced, was much like his own dad: a stern, punishing, authoritarian father-figure, just waiting for you to get out of line in order to discipline you back toward righteousness and repentance.

It was on that otherwise unremarkable Sunday morning that this thirteen-year-old boy first discovered he was an abomination to his Creator. Thumbing randomly through

1

the King James Bible resting on his lap, he happened to
stumble across a verse he'd never seen before (Deut. 22:5,
to be precise), one that caused a spasm of terror in his
heart. The scripture read, "The woman shall not wear that
which pertaineth unto a man, neither shall a man put on
a woman's garment: for all that do so are an abomination
unto the Lord thy God." Cold chills ran down the boy's
spine, for he was certain that this passage was directed
specifically at him.

For some time he'd been secretly dressing in his mother's
and sister's clothing when he was left alone at home, feeling
somehow complete when he did so. Wearing that clothing
brought about an intangible sense of wholeness and seren-
ity, and he always looked forward to those opportunities
when he could enjoy the sensations, even if it was only
for a little while. He never told anyone about his activity, intuitively understanding that he would probably get
in some serious trouble if he spoke of it. He was truly
sorry that he had to use his mother's and his sister's clothes
(how he wished he could have feminine clothing of his
own!). He knew they would be angry if they found out, so
there was a tinge of guilt attached to the behavior. Nevertheless, he still loved the way his crossdressing made him
feel. It was as if he were able, in some mystical way, to
transcend his mundane, everyday masculine self by putting
on the "uniform" of a woman and becoming something
more. Now, however, all that had changed in one fate-
ful instant: God apparently abhorred him because of what
he did.

That boy spent the next two and a half decades struggling
with the enormous guilt created by his legalistic, shame-
based interpretation of this singular passage of Deuteronomic scripture on that hot Sunday morning in central
Florida. He knew instinctively that he had a strong internal feminine component, one that actively craved outward,
physical expression through crossdressing. However, he
also knew that his fundamentalist church and conserva-

tive religious belief system absolutely condemned such behaviors, considering them in the same category as the unspeakably abhorrent sin of homosexuality. After all, everyone knew that God loathed homosexuals and damned them unequivocally to hell.

This child began to develop a sense that something was terribly wrong with him, and he couldn't even talk to anyone about it. Who could he approach: his pastor, his Sunday school teacher, his parents? None of them, he was certain, would have understood or helped him deal with his questions and concerns about his feminine desires. If anything, they would have punished him or sent him away somewhere to be "corrected." People fear what they don't understand, and when they don't understand they turn to their (often incorrect) assumptions.

As time went on the boy would occasionally succumb to his strong and innate desire to crossdress, but he was always filled with guilt, remorse, and repentance afterward. It was not until he was in his middle thirties that he began openly questioning the inflexible, judgmental, shame-based, and soul-killing system of social and religious belief that had held him a prisoner for so many years.

As it happens, every word of this story is true, for I was that guilt-ridden and fearful crossdressing boy. Christian Burgess writes, "Some say that oppression based on sex and gender is at the root of all our society's evils. If this is true, then it is surely our youth that are suffering the most, for it is often too difficult for them to speak for themselves."[1] As a youth and young adult, I suffered because of my feelings of difference. Today I am a proud, healthy, and very happily transgendered person, but that was not always so. I had to walk through the fires of my own shame and inner spiritual condemnation before I could begin to develop a genuine sense of acceptance and pride in who and what I am. It took many years for me to understand that my transgendered orientation is neither a curse nor a sordid temptation from the jaws of hell, but is instead a gift from my loving Creator, and that it is up to me to recognize, embrace, and utilize this divine gift accordingly.

Two of the first things we learn about human beings in the book of Genesis are (1) we are created in the image of God, and (2) we have gender. I'm convinced that these two pieces of information are critical for us if we are to better comprehend the fascinating diversity inherent in the human condition. In these pages I want to focus particularly upon the idea of gender as an integral element of our essential humanity and thus of our relationship to God and to each other. It's true that our individual concepts of gender are primarily derived from strong cultural influences. However, I've learned from research, long-term observation, and personal experience that little if any of what we are taught about gender is actually carved in stone. There are just too many variables. Gender is a social given for each of us in this world, but the ways in which we express and embody the various aspects of gender may (and often do) vary significantly from person to person and culture to culture. Transgendered expression is an important reminder to us all of the inherent and thoroughly delightful possibilities that our human, socialized concept of gender has to offer.

As I began to address my own differently gendered orientation from an adult perspective, I was also forced to confront the reality of my spiritual status before God as a gender variant person. That was no easy task; I had much socialized preconditioning and many faulty beliefs to overcome. In his book *The Four Agreements,* spiritual teacher and author Don Miguel Ruiz states, "We need a great deal of courage to challenge our own beliefs. Because even if we know we didn't choose all these beliefs, it is also true that we agreed to all of them. The agreement is so strong that even if we understand the concept of it not being true, we feel the blame, the guilt, and the shame that occur if we go against these rules."[2] I don't believe I'm particularly courageous, but I had to completely reconsider and reassess my Christian belief system from the ground up. I began to understand that I had accumulated and accepted many potentially false religious assumptions about my personal relationship to God in Christ Jesus. Admitting that truth to myself was frightening yet somehow very liberating; it shook the pillars of my fundamentalist upbringing to their core, and that was healthy. It also allowed me to purposely begin the construction of a newer and more mature system of Christian belief, one based on research, empirical evidence, spiritual honesty, and valid personal experience rather than hearsay, secondhand information, or the biblical literalist and patriarchal pedagogy of the well-intentioned but often misguided Southern Baptist Sunday school teachers of my youth.

This sometimes painful, but necessary and ultimately liberating, evaluation of my Christianity eventually helped me to better understand that I am a unique person, fearfully and wonderfully created in God's image, and I am loved and accepted by God *because* of what I am, not in spite of it. That awareness didn't arrive full-blown overnight but was instead the product of an ongoing effort to learn and grow in my Christian spirituality. I know now that being differently gendered is a remarkable gift and a blessing, not a curse, and I am grateful for God's divine acceptance.

I have also learned that some people, and especially some conservative-evangelical Christians, have a real problem with transgendered folks. The mass media don't seem to help much, either. They almost invariably portray us in a manner that is sensationalistic, and our lives and experiences are often dismissed as trivial or inconsequential. I'm well aware that even some lesbian, gay, and bisexual persons feel that transgendered people are an irritant, a bad joke, an affront to their sensibilities, and a detriment to their movement for equality and civil rights in this country. I understand and appreciate those concerns; they may even have some legitimacy. However, I can tell you from personal experience that we who are differently gendered are people of flesh and blood just like you; we have spiritual needs and concerns just like you; most of us care about

living our lives quietly with dignity and integrity just like
you; and, consequently, we deserve respect and acceptance
just like you.

DEALING WITH DIFFERENCE

The Body of Christ has a God-given ethical and moral
imperative to do justice in this world. Given that responsibility, we who claim the name "Christian" must continually
reassess our own attitudes toward those who are different from us: Do we treat others in an inclusive, loving,
Christ-like manner or do we shun them because of fear
and ignorance? More to the point, are we actively and in-
clusively creating justice in Christ's name or are we simply
playing at religion, giving lip service to Jesus' amazing example of inclusivity and acceptance for all who desire to
know God?

Transgendered people are living proof and constant reminders to us all that there is more than one way to *be* in
this world. I am totally convinced that our Creator absolutely loves and delights in diversity. Just think of all the
different types of plants, animals, terrain, and natural won-
ders on the earth; then remind yourself of all the different
stars in the skies (*billions* and *billions* of them, as Carl Sagan
used to say). Look, too, at the differences that abound even
within the human family: skin color, hair and eye color,
body shapes and weights, facial features, levels of intelli-
gence, talents, abilities, desires, orientations, strengths, and
weaknesses. How could anyone deny that our God absolutely revels in diversification throughout the entire created
universe? Truly, it is creation's diversity that is its glory
and its strength and that most fully reflects the character of its Creator. It is clear that if the Christian church
authentically cares about reflecting and embodying the characteristics of God, then it must also welcome, embrace, and
even insist upon that same divinely created diversity among
its membership. As church we are called to make a deter-

mined effort to be co-creators with God, reaching out in love and mutuality to differently gendered people, thereby drawing them ever closer into an inclusive and caring circle of faith.

It is incumbent upon the Body of Christ to act appropriately and responsibly with compassion, respect, acceptance, and love toward all individuals. Jesus himself taught and always demonstrated that no religious law or doctrine is as important as the law of love. James Cone, professor of systematic theology at Union Theological Seminary, tells us that if the church refuses to extend love and acceptance to all, and particularly to the community of the oppressed, it is acting heretically, not to mention diametrically contrary to the words and intentions of Christ, who said in Matthew 11:28, "Come unto me, all ye who are weary and heavy-laden, and I will give you rest." Jesus didn't say he would give rest to some or only to a privileged, exclusive few who meet some social or religious criteria. He said *all*. That means you and I and everyone else who wants to come to God, without limitation or reservation.

In the view of some, the term "transgendered Christian" is an oxymoron, a contradiction in terms, something like "humility contest." Nevertheless, I'm very pleased to identify myself as both transgendered and Christian. It's not always easy to be both and to stay within the church, but it's worth it to me. I have come to understand that there's nothing wrong or sinful about being a transgendered Christian, but there's something highly amiss with a Christian community that cannot love, accept, and respect good people who happen to be differently gendered. The manner in which any social or religious institution responds to the community of the oppressed is usually an effective measure of its social and spiritual maturity, not to mention its authenticity and viability as an agent of good in this world. I hope to be one of many who struggle to create a transformative difference inside the church, provoking and goading it lovingly but unceasingly toward an ever-increasing understanding and a welcoming, affirming attitude extended to all people in Jesus' holy name.

We who are Christian and transgendered must learn to use and depend upon the Bible as a textbook for our own spiritual liberation. Paul's Letter to the Romans reminds us that "not just the children of God" but all of "creation itself, groaning in labor pains, will be set free from its bondage" (Rom. 8:22). Despite the exclusive, unjust and discriminatory interpretations of the Bible that many of us learned while growing up, the scriptures can truly become a hopeful, inspiring, liberating word of freedom and redemption for our souls if we learn where and how to look for that liberation. The salvific, redemptive love and acceptance of God really *is* there in the Bible for anyone who desires a close, personal relationship with the Creator. We should *never* let anyone use the Bible to oppress us. William Sloane Coffin said: "Altogether too many Christians, even scholarly ones, use the Bible as a drunk does a lamp post: for support rather than for illumination."

I grew up fearing, despising, rejecting, and running from the fact that I'm a differently gendered person, and my self-loathing almost destroyed me until the transcendent love of God eventually allowed me to learn that being differently gendered is indeed a wonderful blessing and a marvelous opportunity for personal discovery. Psychiatry's Diagnostic and Statistical Manual can rattle on all it wants about "gender dysphoria"; I'm now convinced that my status should instead be labeled "gender euphoria." Recognizing our worthy uniqueness as people of God is wondrous and blessed. God has given remarkable gifts to each of us in different ways, and it's our responsibility as Christians to discern and then use those gifts to help serve and liberate others in Jesus' name. In these pages we will discuss the concepts of spiritual growth and freedom as they apply to the differently gendered and to the church, for both communities are in need of the joyful, liberating message of God's love and salvation in this hurting world.

CALLED TO TRANSFORMATION
AND LIBERATION

Part of my purpose in writing this book is to help raise the consciousness of the church about these matters and therefore, as the tired but useful cliché reminds us, to "comfort the afflicted while afflicting the comfortable." I hope that the institutional church begins to recognize its own need for genuine internal transformation and gender-based liberation so that all people everywhere may fully and equally enjoy the freedoms as well as the important responsibilities that are intrinsic to the Body of Christ.

Even if a transgendered person is not engaging in a particular form of differently gendered behavior or activity on any given day or at any particular time, the social forces of oppression and discrimination are still hard at work around the clock to permeate, negatively inform, and pervasively influence the life of that person. Our culture is fragmented and confused about gender. The result is that transgendered people must continually confront ignorance, fear, and negativity, especially within our religious institutions.

In these pages I will attempt to convey some of the reasons why the development of a transgender-based liberation theology is so essential for the lives of those who deal with Christian spiritual concerns on a daily basis. This book exists because, in the words of liberation theologians Leonardo and Clodovis Boff, "any original theological vision tends, with the passage of time and through its own internal logic, to seek more formal expression. Liberation theology always sets out to reexamine the whole basic content of revelation and tradition so as to bring out the social and liberating dimensions implicit in both sources."[3] In writing this book I often returned to a fundamental question: "What should a specifically transgender-based liberation theology really be about?" The primary answer to that query, I believe, lies in honestly addressing the issue of being "other" or "different" within a society and a religious institution that tends to demand homogeneity, particularly in terms of conforming to specified gender expectations. I want to confront and discuss these issues in a way that helps to foster liberation and create justice for the souls of those who are so oppressed and alienated. Consequently, my most important goal is to offer the hope and salvation that is found only in a relationship with Jesus Christ—and not necessarily within systematic, fixed, or dogmatic religious belief systems—to those who find themselves in such a difficult and undeserved situation.

By definition, and as a matter of plain fact, we transgendered persons do not fit neatly into society's arbitrarily determined categories with regard to gender and are thus considered to be "strangers" or "foreigners" by most of our social institutions, including the church. So, this book is about the struggles and the spiritual journeys of socially perceived "others" or "aliens," transgendered persons who are attempting to personally define and thus develop a more fulfilling relationship with our Creator and with the Christian church in the light of our uniquely transgendered status.

Many people, both outside and within the Christian community, have internalized our culture's arbitrary gender-based norms to such an extent that the mere presence of a recognized differently gendered individual can quickly create intense anxiety or even overt antagonism within them. It is imperative that we who are gender variant help others to overcome their prejudices and bigotries so that legitimate progress toward understanding, acceptance, and mutual respect may become a genuine reality instead of just a hopeful dream. This can be accomplished through educational outreach, altruistic personal interaction, and, perhaps even more importantly, openness, honesty, and integrity in our daily lives. For some of us, this means "coming out" to as many people as we safely can. This is crucial because "the opportunity to tell one's story can be an empowering and healing event. The first-person account also helps shift our attention from pathology to adaptation. When those who literally 'live the life' are willing to speak out," they become effective advocates for themselves and for other differently gendered persons.[4] There is an edifying and transformative power that is manifested in coming out to others. I've witnessed it repeatedly. The more people who know us and can see us living honorably and ethically as proud and happily transgendered persons, the better the world becomes for all gender variant people.

I also hope to provide informational assistance to the family members and friends of differently gendered persons. These people often struggle to cope with the uninvited complexities and dilemmas of a loved one's transgender circumstance. They deserve a resource to assist in those struggles, especially when dealing with the spiritual concerns and ramifications of the situation. Finally, I want to help separate fact from fiction with regard to issues of transgendered Christian spirituality. There are far too many misconceptions about this area of human endeavor, so it is important to begin dispelling unfounded myths and replacing them with facts.

Toward those ends, I will examine the complexities of reflecting on gender and faith in contemporary society (chapter 2). I will then outline current understandings of concepts related to gender and transgender and look at the current situation of the transgendered individual in society (chapters 3 and 4). Next I will briefly consider some of the social, political, and religious factors that have historically shaped our culture's negative attitudes toward the transgendered in our midst (chapter 5). As an extension of that discussion I include a chapter dealing with the autobiographical accounts of several transgendered persons, narratives that express the human struggles and discoveries that almost invariably accompany a differently gendered status (chapter 6). Following that, I will submit an admittedly controversial proposal for consideration: the Christian church is struggling mightily with its own distinct, uniquely

transgendered essence. I will offer evidence for this perhaps
surprising premise and will briefly discuss the reasons for
and the nature of the church's struggles with this issue.
Further developing this line of thought regarding the existence and importance of a transgendered spiritual essence
within the Christian church, I will examine some of the
characteristic behaviors that society attributes to males and
females and will then reflect upon those very behaviors as
they were manifested and exhibited in the exemplary life of
Jesus Christ (chapter 7).

Having thus constructed a framework for our consideration of the liberative importance of the Gospel in the lives
of transgendered persons, I will discuss the multifaceted
nature of that liberation as it pertains to the existence
and cultural status of differently gendered Christians (chapter 8). Then I will propose a positive, life-giving alternative
to the perpetuation and maintenance of oppressive, un-
Christian paradigms and behaviors within the church that
have historically been directed toward the gender variant. This negativity includes attitudes and actions such
as transgenderphobia, bigotry and prejudice, xenophobia,
exclusivity, etc., on the part of some members of the institutional church. The positive alternative of which I speak
is to be found, of course, in a greater understanding of
the liberating Gospel of Jesus Christ as it offers hope,
freedom, justice, dignity, and salvation for the lives of transgendered persons and for all people. I will also offer a
brief series of steps to help differently gendered persons
move toward greater, more enriching spiritual awareness
(chapter 9).

Next, I will consider the nature of the ongoing struggle
for transgendered inclusion within the church (chapter 10).
Part of this chapter deals with the work of creating justice,
followed by an analysis of the church's traditionally androcentric, power-based paradigm of fear. The final chapter
(chapter 11) includes a discussion of the concepts of heresy
as it relates to gender variant Christians and takes a look at

the spiritual needs of transgendered persons. The book concludes with hopes and prayers for progress in the spiritual pursuit of justice for gender variant people.

CONFRONTING A MINDSET
OF FEAR

While some who call themselves "Christian" would much prefer that transgendered individuals simply go away or not exist at all, it is equally true that not every Christian is antagonistic or hostile toward differently gendered persons, at least in my experience. I remain convinced that it is only a tiny percentage of people who display overt animosity or hatred toward the transgendered. This negative temperament of which I speak is simply a mean-spirited attitude, one usually based upon a literalist or fundamentalist ideology, a mindset too often rooted in fear, misinformation, and an inaccurate biblical hermeneutic with regard to the differently gendered.

Most people are simply more just and loving toward others than that, regardless of their biblical interpretive stance. I have personally witnessed and experienced many acts of love, compassion, respect, acceptance, and mutuality extended toward transgendered people by both clergy and laity. I certainly approve of and encourage such attitudes and behaviors on the part of Christians everywhere and, based on what I know about the Savior, I have absolutely no doubt that it is what Jesus would do. It remains abundantly clear, though, that there has been a depressingly lengthy history of oppression and marginalization directed toward those whom the church views or designates as "different" (which is, unfortunately, often equated with "inferior," "wrong," or "sinful").

Differently gendered persons have long been convenient scapegoats for those whose bigotry, prejudice, and exclusivist theologies are cloaked in the guise of religious piety. We are essentially pushed to the periphery of our faith communities, and the institutional church likes to pretend that we don't exist. Even when the fact of our existence is grudgingly admitted, we are usually treated pejoratively with pity, disdain, ridicule, and misunderstanding. Gender variant people deserve none of that. Such actions and attitudes ultimately harm everyone, because "discrimination, oppression, and prejudice directed against any group is damaging to the social, emotional, and economic well-being of the affected group, as well as to society as a whole."[5]

The institution of Christianity has usually been quick and perhaps even overly eager to assign transgendered people to such negative and undeserved categories. Due primarily to the variations on traditional social gender roles that differently gendered people so often embody, we have been historically perceived as sexually or morally "deviant" by the church—and therefore somehow "deficient" or "unworthy" as human beings. That perception is not accurate, just, or Christlike, and such an attitude is in desperate need of transformation. Of course, we must remember that acceptance, respect, affirmation, and love for the differently gendered within the church is a new paradigm for some of us, and anything new is often feared and dreaded.

One objective of this book is to avoid personally attacking or demonizing people (though unjust attitudes, philosophies, and actions are fair game). I am not interested in dragging others through the mud, nor do I wish to assume the role of judge with regard to other human beings. I have no authority to condemn other individuals; judgment is God's job, not mine.

The enemy we are confronting is *evil* in its various manifestations, not people, and certainly not our Christian sisters and brothers. I desire only to realistically discuss the difficulties that confront transgendered Christians in today's world, and then to offer these persons legitimate hope and a way to move toward God's love and justice through the mechanism of a transgender-based liberation theology. To quote Carter Heyward,

We have an enemy, but the enemy is not "them," not "those others." The enemy is . . . not right wing, racist, heterosexist Christian individuals. We need to see that our enemy is neither "us" nor "them," but rather is the alienated power relations cemented in fear, much of it our own. It is against the alienation that festers between us that we need to contend. This enemy belongs to us all. It is transpersonal in that it affects everyone and cannot be pinned down, permanently, on anyone.[6]

Transgendered people have long been denied the opportunity to exist and operate in right relationship with the Christian church, due primarily to the "alienated power relations cemented in fear" existing on both sides of this unfortunate equation. It is my hope that this book will in some way help to explain and overcome that environment of fear so that healthy and right relations may once again be established between members of God's beloved human family.

I also want to make it clear that, while I have been heavily influenced by the work of Christian liberation and feminist theologians, this book should in no way be construed as an attempt to co-opt or misuse the writings, the experiences, or the struggles of others who have done important theological work before me. We all stand on the shoulders of those who have gone before us, and I am certainly no exception to that rule. I am deeply indebted to many wonderful writers and theologians of various backgrounds and fields of expertise who have paved the way and thus provided inspiration, insight, and hope for the church, for the transgender community, and for me as an individual. I freely admit that my thoughts and ideas are not wholly original, nor did they occur in a vacuum; after all, there really is nothing new under the sun. Instead, I am the synthesized product, for better or worse, of all my lifetime experiences and myriad influences, and I want to give credit where it is due. However, in this book I seek to be as nonderivative as possible by confining my focus to the uniquely transgendered Christian experience, an experience that I am living out on a daily basis. I hope that my purposely specific approach to this subject matter may also paradoxically achieve a more universal application, particularly in those matters that concern the human issues of freedom, personal dignity, respect, acceptance, and love for all of God's creation.

YOUR INVITATION

It is inevitable that different people will respond to a book like this in different ways; I'm well aware that it's impossible to please everyone. Some will undoubtedly reject the book and its message outright. Some will probably consider this work to be shallow, offensive, or less than authoritative. Others will take umbrage with the content, the subject matter, or the construction of my assertions and contentions. To those persons I can only reply that this is the first book of its kind; it's a beginning, a starting point. It may or may not meet your scholarly, theological, philosophical, ideological, sociopolitical, or personal criteria, but it is at least an initial attempt to make a positive difference for transgendered persons and for the Christian church. Some may discover various items of interest or value in these pages while dismissing other parts of the work. (Please, as members of Twelve-Step groups often say, "take what you like and leave the rest.") I hope that many will find this book to be a valuable tool and a legitimate resource to which they may turn repeatedly for assistance and encouragement in their struggles for justice and personal and community liberation. If nothing else, I hope that all who read these words may become better informed about the spiritual, social, and political difficulties that many transgendered persons confront each day.

Education about a specific issue usually creates a more generalized awareness, which potentially can lead to increased knowledge and human wisdom. Greater wisdom, in turn, can engender compassion, and compassion can evolve into genuine relationship rooted in mutuality. It is my desire that each of us, no matter what our gender or sexual orientation may be, might come to a place of greater knowledge, wisdom, compassion, acceptance, and Christian love for our transgendered sisters and brothers.

As we begin our journey toward that sacred destination, I invite my readers to carefully consider the words in this book. Are they reasonable? Are they accurate? Are they based upon opinion, experience, research, or combinations of all these factors? Are they consistent with your own experience, knowledge, and beliefs? Why or why not? You are certainly free to disagree with any or all of the stated ideas in these pages but, if you differ with me, I hope you will at least base your arguments on something other than a generalized feeling or an emotionally derived and out-of-context biblical response to a perceived situation. If you choose to disagree, that's fine—but please be specific and bring some legitimate rationale for your argument to the table of discussion. I do not consider prooftexting, taking specific biblical passages out of their appropriate historical and spiritual context to "prove" one's position on a particular issue, to be a proper or just mechanism for a fair assessment of any spiritual matter. These concerns are more important than that—we're talking about people's *lives*—and they subsequently deserve careful, thoughtful, compassionate consideration.

It may appear to some that this book dwells primarily upon negativities, but this is not my intention. Nevertheless, I am convinced it is necessary to stress the need for a heightened awareness of the injustices that have been and continue to be perpetrated upon transgendered people by society as a whole, and certainly by the institution of the Christian church. The Body of Christ has wounded and oppressed the differently gendered. Even worse, the church continues to do so, and to ignore that fact would be cavalier. However, my real focus in these pages is always upon the myriad possibilities for enrichment created by the presence, contributions, and active involvement of transgendered persons within Christianity. I'm no Pollyanna, but I am an optimist by nature. I fully expect that one day the differently gendered will be totally included in the central life of the church, without reservation.

You may be asking yourself, "Why should she be so optimistic? Upon what does she base her hope, and how can she be so confident of an ultimate success for all of God's people?" My answer is twofold: first, I am convinced that a greater understanding of accurate information and theological principles will inevitably lead to a lessening of socioreligious hostilities toward the gender variant as well as other gender/sexual minorities and oppressed groups. Knowledge lessens fear, and a cessation of fear offers the possibility of positive change, change that can allow the Christian community to move past its current prejudices and bigotries. Second, I am convinced and have seen strong evidence that God is actively working in the hearts and minds of transgendered and nontransgendered persons alike to bring about reconciliation and healing within the Body of Christ. One day, hopefully in the not-too-distant future, the Christian church, along with the rest of society, will begin to realize and accept the fact that being differently gendered is *not* a "choice," a "preference," or a "lifestyle": it is an orientation, a blessed gift from our Creator. Gender variance is a fundamental component of some human beings' natural, God-given makeup in much the same way that some people are left- or right-brained, left- or right-handed, or red- or blond-haired. The church must begin to understand that God does not favor those who have certain skin colors or hairlines or genitalia or body weights or IQ's or sexual orientations or gender orientations—God loves and accepts us all equally, desiring a relationship with each one of us.

There are those who would tell you that I am a freak of some sort because I am a transgendered person. And I've been called worse! Over the years I have learned that being "different" is not only acceptable but can actually be very good, even blessed and holy. Besides, much like transgender activist Kate Bornstein, "I realized that, yep, I was a freak all right, but I was only a freak to the degree that I remained silent. When I spoke, I had a chance to educate, and, paradoxically, I became less of a freak."[7] Personally, I shudder at the thought of being a cookie-cutter clone who unequivocally accepts religious teaching, doctrine, or dogma without question or reflection. I value my spiritual autonomy and individuality, especially as they pertain to my personal relationship, rooted in mutuality, with Jesus Christ. We Christians needn't fear asking questions or reconsidering aspects of our faith; if our Christian beliefs are real, vital, and relevant to our lives then they can surely stand up to some questioning and even skepticism. And if they can't, then we don't have much of a belief system anyway.

2

CONFRONTING THE COMPLEXITIES OF DIFFERENCE AND FAITH

I AM A BELIEVER in the good news, the "liberating word" of the Gospel of Jesus Christ. However, I am not at all convinced that our human spirituality is necessarily best served by attempting to solve, once and for all, the eternal mystery of God. I'm far from the first to come to that realization; Chuang-tzu, a Chinese philosopher and teacher of the fourth century B.C.E., said, "If the great Way is made clear, it is not the Way." Our spirituality and our theology are most effective when healthily devoted to contemplating, appreciating, celebrating, loving, and simply being open to God's profound, inexplicable mystery. It seems to me that such an important endeavor must necessarily include a legitimate consideration of, and respect for, the many ways in which human beings—all of whom are created in God's image, the *imago Dei*—may variously manifest that divine image.

CONSIDERING DIFFERENCE

Diversity, pluralism, multiculturalism: these are often difficult issues with which to struggle in our fragmented society, but the effort to intentionally invite those concepts into the fabric of our lives will inevitably enrich our existence, give us greater insight into the wonderful variety that exists in God's creation, and ultimately allow us who call ourselves

Christian to more fully embody the compassionate love of Jesus toward all persons. Such an important enterprise must surely result in an increased state of spiritual liberation for each of us as individuals and for the Christian church as a whole. Liberation of this sort will, in turn, allow us to more abundantly experience the richness and fulfillment that a life lived in right relationship with God and with each other has to offer. This book is written in an attempt to nurture and encourage those healthy and sacred pursuits.

Part of any effort to consider the potential diversity that human beings represent ought to include thinking about—and again, celebrating—both our differences and our similarities as naturally occurring, historically relevant parts of our lives on this earth. For followers of Jesus Christ this effort must, of necessity, entail a careful consideration of the effects of Christian absolutist orthodox beliefs. That in turn may require a genuine and perhaps even painful (yet potentially life-giving and ultimately rewarding) reassessment of the place of such beliefs in the lives of thinking Christians. As we do so we must keep in mind that "absolutist orthodoxies have contributed untold pain on world history. Today, they are no less threatening in their various Christian, Islamic or Jewish forms than they were in the 15th century when the Council of Florence declared that outside of the Church there is no salvation, which resulted in the Jews being expelled from Spain or tortured into Catholic conversion."[1] From such potentially dangerous absolutist belief systems have arisen crusades, jihads, inquisitions, pogroms, gay/lesbian/bisexual/transgender bashing, misogyny, sexism, enforced heterosexism, institutionalized racism and slavery, violent and imperialistic evangelicalism, patriarchy, and other forms of socioreligious oppression.

We need to be continually reminded that "it has been the case in history that the dominant groups always claim that their views are universal."[2] Typically, then, it is always the ones in positions of power who formulate and enforce

the rules (and who write the history books). Those in the
social or religious center often have the arbitrary privilege
of claiming and enforcing absolutism with regard to their
stated beliefs, and that can become very dangerous for persons who have been banished to the margins of our social
institutions.

OUR IMAGES OF GOD

I now wish to offer what some may consider to be a controversial and perhaps even heretical thesis: when considering
the often difficult and certainly complex situation of differently gendered Christians, the lives and welfare of human
beings are ultimately more important than any orthodox religious doctrines or ideologies created by and for society and
its institutions, no matter how well-intentioned, popular, or
well-established those ideologies or doctrines may be. Jesus
appeared to have no problem with this concept at all. After
all, Jesus was the one who informed us that the Sabbath
was made for humankind, not humankind for the Sabbath
(Mark 2:27). The implication for us today is that religious
and spiritual guidelines should always be designed and im-
plemented to help persons live into their full individual
potential. Such guidelines must never become a hindrance
or a stumbling block to people in their journey through
life because, as Jesus so wisely demonstrated, people are ultimately more important than rules. People are created in
the image of God—and rules are not. Socioreligious guidelines, doctrines, and dogma invariably become idolatrous
whenever they are elevated in importance above the human
beings they were intended to help and serve.

Our notions of God totally affect the way we view the
world and organize our lives.[3] We therefore owe it to God
and ourselves to pursue as clear and unfettered a perspective
of our Creator as possible and to always be open to new
possibilities for reimagining God as a manifested presence
in our lives. Absolutist views of God are, in themselves, al-

ways limiting and counterproductive. Such views put God in a box, creating inflexible constructs around one's idea of who and what God is, and when that happens the potential for relationship between an infinite God and finite humans is always impaired and diminished. If we can learn to move beyond such ineffective and incomplete absolutist paradigms, then we may also begin to experience the presence of God in new, exciting, and spiritually liberating ways.

Speaking of the dangerous ideology of religious absolutism, Rev. Philip Wogaman, noted Christian ethicist and pastor of Foundry United Methodist Church in Washington, D.C., states, "The only absolute is God and...when humans make absolutes out of a 'cultural expression' such as heterosexuality...then they have succumbed to 'idolatry.'"[4] Our culture has indeed made idols of various "expressions" on many levels, sex and gender expectations ranking high among them. Although Wogaman's statement refers to his views on heterosexuality, I believe that the issue of transgendered expression and behavior could (and should) be an important addendum to his idea. Besides, as author Pat Califia reminds us, "We understand so very little that any claim to authority is premature. The best we can do is speak our own truth, make it safe for others to speak theirs, and respect our differences."[5]

Our culture has created and avidly enforces specific, yet highly arbitrary, rules regarding gender-based behavior and appearance. These social expectations have taken on the force of absolutes, especially as they pertain to those who differ from the statistical norm in terms of their gender orientation. Such a rigid, intractable approach to this complex issue is surely detrimental to the lives and healthy self-images of transgendered people (and, ultimately, to everyone else), as socioreligious idolatry and inflexibility in the face of benign human diversity always is. Since society is collectively composed of individuals, it would appear that our culture does itself a major disservice whenever it denies or invalidates the potential benefits that could ac-

crue through a genuine social acceptance and affirmation
of differently gendered persons.

An awareness of the inevitability of theological ambiguity
is a logical position for any thinking Christian. Absolutist
doctrines or dogma regarding the Creator of the universe
are, at best, incomplete and naïve in their insistence that
they alone are correct, to the exclusion of any contradic-
tory information. Such ideologies are harmful to anyone
who cares about honesty and integrity in terms of theological understanding. (The Scopes "monkey trial" of 1925
turned the teaching of evolution in Tennessee into ban-
ner headlines, sparking courtroom debate as to whether
faith and reason could peacefully coexist. As that historic
event unfolded, it became frighteningly clear that some
people simply don't welcome the intrusion of fact, reality,
human wisdom, or reason into the perceived security of
their absolutist religious beliefs.)

DEVELOPMENT AND DIALOGUE

For many Christians, liberation theologies have come to
symbolize a way for those of us who are somehow "different" (and therefore often dehumanized, marginalized,
excluded, or otherwise oppressed) to better comprehend
and act upon our relationships with God, with the institutional church, and with the sociopolitical environment in
which we find ourselves. The struggle for greater knowledge
about gender variant persons and their spiritual significance
will inevitably continue to engage both society and the
Christian community. For this reason, we need to develop
more comprehensive and insightful theological language so
we can speak with clarity and precision to these important
issues.

Since theology is always contextual, I owe it to my readers to articulate and nuance who and what I am—and
am not. Declaring my own context first limits the scope
of my authority and then, conversely, allows me to write,

speak, and work openly for justice within the Christian church. Like Susan Hill Lindley, professor of religion at St. Olaf College, Northfield, Minnesota, I consider myself to be one who is critical of the institutional church's historical patriarchy and sexism (and heterosexism, racism, misogyny, transgenderphobia, etc.) but who also embraces that same church as a source of meaning and hope.[6] I am white, middle-class, middle-aged, biologically male, North American, Christian, and a male-to-female crossdresser—a proud, happily transgendered person. I am therefore limited in that my personal experiences fall into the above categories. I cannot and do not presume to speak for those whose lives and experiences are different from mine. I am not biologically female, Hispanic, Buddhist, or extremely wealthy. I cannot write as if I were, or as if I could somehow understand or make completely accurate distinctions and assessments about the daily lives and experiences of people in other social, racial, theological, or economic contexts. Nevertheless, I *am* free within my particular contextual sphere to write openly and honestly of my own observations, experiences, and insights from a theological perspective.

I am well aware of the inherent dangers that exist whenever anyone's personal situation or individual beliefs are universalized. Therefore, it is not my intention to speak for everyone, or even for all transgendered Christians. I do not have the right, the calling, the authority, or the ability to do that. I can only speak authentically and legitimately for myself, but in so doing I hope to strike a responsive chord in the hearts and minds of those who are willing to accompany me on this sacred journey.

HISTORIC OPPRESSION

Historically speaking, Christianity and its androcentric, hierarchical power structures have been intimately involved with fomenting injustice toward transgendered persons.

Some of this oppression has been due to a misunderstanding or misinterpretation of the reasons for the existence of an Old Testament injunction against crossdressing found in Deuteronomy 22:5. (We shall discuss that scripture passage and its implications in more detail later on.) Some of it has to do with religio-political maneuvering by the church fathers (mothers with such influence have been historical rarities in the church); this maneuvering was particularly true during the Middle Ages, but such machinations have continued in the church down through the centuries.

In 691 C.E. the Council of Constantinople decreed that "no man shall put on a woman's dress nor a woman, clothes that belong to men." Throughout the Middle Ages the Catholic Church did its best to link transgendered people with witchcraft,[7] and the church even taught that witches had the power to change sex.[8] In 1233 the "Holy" Inquisition began, and transgendered people were made the victims of terror and mass murder by the church in Europe. Joan of Arc was burned at the stake by French Catholic church leaders for, among other things, her insistence upon wearing men's clothing and cutting her hair in a masculine style. Negativity toward the gender variant became an entrenched attitude within the power structures of Christianity, and that attitude has continued to be manifested in various forms. In the United States, for instance, some of those murdered during the Salem witch trials of the late 1600s were transgendered. Today, the list of differently gendered persons attacked, injured, or killed continues to grow.[9] The saddest part is that our religious institutions help create a climate of fear and negativity in which such destructive actions are not only permissible but quietly encouraged.

Many in the institutional church still consider the existence and practices of differently gendered persons to be "abnormal," "sinful," "deviant," and a social, moral, and spiritual danger to Christianity in general. This form of religious oppression has led to incredible amounts of suffering, heartache, spiritual disillusionment, and even suicide by many sexual/gender minority Christians over the centuries. When the considerable power of the church is amassed behind a religious teaching that says one is somehow anathema to God and is therefore intrinsically flawed, it's difficult for the one being maligned to maintain a strong sense of attachment or involvement with such a blatantly hostile institution. Astonishingly, and to their great credit, many transgendered persons continue to be active, albeit mostly closeted, members of mainstream Christian denominations.

Because of this long history of religious oppression it is critical that we who are gender variant begin to develop a Christian theology of our own, a liberative and continually evolving theology that is consistently and necessarily rooted in the experiences and struggles marking the course of our individual and collective differently gendered journeys. We must "do" our theology while being firmly grounded in an experiential authenticity and a historic awareness of our own transgendered existence.

3

CLARIFYING GENDER AND TRANSGENDER

A T LEAST SOME READERS will need and perhaps appreciate a bit of basic information regarding the nature of the transgender phenomenon itself. If you're like most people you know relatively little about the topic, and what you do know is perhaps inaccurate or has been severely warped through the lens of the popular media's distortions and sensationalism. We need to circumvent the "circus" so that we can begin learning the truth, a truth based in reality and personal experience rather than sensationalistic ploys for media ratings or cant in the service of socioreligious power. Unfortunately, according to college professor and GenderTalk radio talk show host Gordene O. MacKenzie,

> the abundance of demeaning images and stereotypes of [transgendered persons] found in American popular culture reinforces their social and personal stigmatization and inequality. Since most of these images are media generated and reach large audiences, they have the power not only to reflect culturally biased beliefs about gender but also the potential to shape them. In most cases, sensationalized media portrayals of transgenderists have little to do with the day-to-day reality of most transgenderists and everything to do with the ratings and sales of popular cultural products featuring transgenderists.[1]

Tabloid television shows, while certainly popular and able to achieve high ratings (while raking in the almighty dollar accordingly), usually do the transgender community a disservice by presenting a grossly distorted picture of the real lives and issues of differently gendered persons. Gerald Mallon, author and social service worker, states:

> News stories and talk shows in the mass media are often less than objective and in many cases replete with inaccuracies.... The media, especially the talk-show circuit—Jerry Springer, Ricki Lake, Sally Jesse Raphael, Jenny Jones, and others—have all made a great deal of money by sensationalizing the stories of individuals who are somewhere on the transgender spectrum.[2]

Such shows generally do much more harm than good. "For the most part, they only impart misinformation and perpetuate myths."[3] The vast majority of transgendered people would never consider appearing on such programs. Our lives are not ridiculous parodies of human relationships, and most of us are not clowns, fools, or sad, deluded persons who are pathetically desperate for our allotted fifteen minutes of "fame."

Because many people in our society possess little or no awareness of the complexities and the very real, non-sensationalistic issues that concern transgendered persons, I offer the following brief introduction to the subject. The information presented here is not intended to be a complete or comprehensive examination of the transgender phenomenon. Even so, I hope to provide at least a limited frame of reference for our study of transgendered Christian spirituality.

ON GENDER

Initially, and for the sake of clarity, we need to determine what we mean by "gender." "Gender is 'read' by others on

the basis of gender attributes that we convey."[4] Gordene
MacKenzie tells us,

> Every day we do gender. The way we look, the way
> we act, dress, talk, walk, wear our hair, think about
> ourselves, communicate with others and desire com-
> prise our gender schema. Gender is one of the most
> common daily rituals performed. It is also one of the
> most effective means of social control. From birth we
> are enculturated into a dual gender system, reinforced
> by all the major institutions.[5]

We will discuss this controlling, bipolar, ubiquitous, and
extremely rigid system of socialized gender expectations in
more detail as this book unfolds.

To further clarify our basic perspective on gender, let us
consider the words of Kate Bornstein:

> Gender is real easy to sum up in one word: catego-
> rization. Anything that categorizes people is gender,
> whether it's appearance or mannerisms, biology or
> psychology, hormones, roles, genitals, whatever: if
> we're trying to categorize or separate people out, it's
> gender.[6]

Scientifically speaking, one's gender identity may have
little or nothing to do with one's sexual orientation. Although there may be some overlap, gender identity is
usually much more concerned with one's psychological,
emotional, and spiritual internal essence and self-awareness
than one's anatomical structure or sexual attractions. Many
transgendered persons feel as though they have a different,
internally manifested gender than that which may be indi-
cated by their genes, body types, or sexual organs. John
Money states:

> Although they are used carelessly and synonymously,
> sex and gender are not synonymous. They are also not
> antonyms, although they are frequently used almost as

if they were. In one such usage, sex is defined as what you are born with, as male or female, and gender is what you acquire as a social role, from a social script.[7]

Crudely put: "Sex deals with what's between your legs, and gender with what's between your ears."

Society expects us to adopt certain gender roles based upon our bodies. Those expectations are usually predicated upon our genitalia and begin from the moment of birth, continuing throughout our lives. When, for whatever reason, someone doesn't meet these anatomically based gender expectations, the result is often a psychological, emotional, spiritual, and physical conundrum. In a sermon at a seminary chapel service, female-to-male transsexual Patrick Gambill-Read put it this way:

"Is it a boy or a girl?" The first question that everybody asks when a baby is born. Even the folks in the delivery room. And how does that question get answered? Visually. By a very quick look at the baby's outsides. But when we start to unravel gender—what makes any of us male or female, or none of the above, or all of the above—we start to realize that it's social, economic, political, cultural, emotional, interpersonal; it's way, way more than physical sex. And physical sex, in turn, is a lot more than what's visible on a newborn baby's outsides. Physical sex includes our hormones, chromosomes, brain and body chemistry during pregnancy, what's inside and invisible as well as what's visible on the outside. So there's an awful lot of data that cursory inspection in the delivery room can't possibly take into consideration in answering that first question. Now, for many if not most of us, that additional data is consistent with what's visible on our outsides. But, for a number of us, the data is mixed. Heart and spirit tell us one thing and culture, based on looking at the outside, tells us the opposite.[8]

Freud insisted that anatomy is destiny, but transgendered people all over the world are proving Freud wrong on a daily basis. Freud's dictum, writes J. J. Allen, "while true in its time, is now a non sequitur, for it doesn't logically follow that a penis or a vagina should predetermine a role in life. No person, man or woman, should have to live a life based upon a roll of the dice that took place at conception."[9] And that's essentially because "a person's gender identity does not always conform to her or his gender at birth."[10] Still, society has a hard time understanding and dealing with those who don't fit neatly into those convenient masculine/feminine boxes of gender dimorphism that are so culturally ingrained. This can, in turn, make it extremely difficult for a gender variant person to achieve a healthy sense of self-esteem and personal acceptance; the powerful, ubiquitous forces of social expectation and disapproval are working against them.

According to Ken Cooper, "Despite these cultural prescriptions, our wider experience tells us that neither sex nor gender are bi-polar, inevitably correlated, and invariant."[11] The very existence of differently gendered persons seems to create questions that are simply not part of the picture for most people: "Few of us question the assignment that was made at birth. Fewer still question the meaning of the question. Must we be a boy or a girl? Are these the only two options? Are they mutually distinguishable, or do we have a choice in the matter?"[12] Consideration of questions like these is simply outside the realm of most people's experience. Yet, for the gender variant person, such questions are fundamental in terms of gender identity development and understanding.

A person who is transgendered usually feels a strong need to express an inner psychological profile that is opposite or at least different in some way from that person's anatomical sex. For many transgendered persons (but certainly not all; sweeping generalizations can often be very inaccurate) this desire for personal gender variant expression is accomplished through dressing and/or behaving as a member of the opposite sex. "In a world that insists on the duality and consistency of sex and gender, coming to understand transgenderism is a challenge."[13] To better comprehend what this challenge entails, let us briefly examine a few of the ways in which transgendered people meet their internal need to express and experience a differently gendered yet completely valid and important component of themselves.

TRANSGENDERED EMBODIMENTS

A *crossdresser* is, quite simply, one who dresses in the clothing of the other gender, as gender is defined by society. Such a person lives most of his or her life within the limits of a culturally assigned masculine or feminine gender role, but has a strong internal need to express an "opposite" side by periodically wearing the clothing and/or attempting to behave as a member of the "other" gender.[14] Research on file with the International Foundation for Gender Education in Waltham, Massachusetts, indicates that the majority of transgendered persons probably fall under the very broad heading of "crossdresser."[15] Totally accurate classification of such a complex issue is problematic at best; gender-based categories can and often do overlap to varying degrees.

As with so many sex- and gender-related cultural scenarios, a grossly unfair double standard exists regarding crossdressing. Women are relatively free to wear men's clothing in our society, and there are some nontranssexual women who prefer to dress, behave, and be perceived solely and exclusively as males. Consequently, the majority of persons considered to be "crossdressers" (and who are therefore easy targets for ridicule and stigmatization) are biologically male. The entertainment industry has known this for a long time. A man in a dress guarantees a cheap laugh.

In some transgender people the dominant internalized gender is so strongly manifested that a condition of dysphoria (or dis-ease) may occur. This situation is sometimes diagnosed by the psychiatric community as *gender identity disorder,* or *GID.* (It should be noted that many persons in the transgender community feel that such a clinical description or medical diagnosis is highly unfair, and active attempts are being made to alter the *DSM-IV*'s diagnostic approach to this area of concern.) When this situation exists, it may eventually prove necessary for these persons to live partly or even entirely as members of the opposite gender in order to relieve the negative, stressful effects of denying or repressing their strong internal need.

Not all those who live in such a manner, however, do so because of a perceived or manifested gender dis-ease. They may very healthily and happily decide to live that way simply because they like it and because it suits them to do so. Those who choose to live full-time in the role of the opposite gender without sexual reassignment surgery (regardless of their motivations) are called *transgenderists.* Both male and female transgenderists exist, although due to a lack of research we are able to estimate only roughly the actual numbers of such persons.

In a relatively small percentage of cases, the gender-based discomfort is so intense that the only way to resolve the gender conflict is to undergo hormone therapy and/or sexual reassignment surgery in order to make the physical body conform more closely to the internalized psychological gender. This situation is usually referred to as *transsexualism.* It is, quite obviously, a highly intense form of transgender expression. There is something extremely profound, even mystical and quintessentially life changing, about a decision to completely alter one's anatomical sex in order to be more congruent with an internalized, gender-based psychological awareness or perception of the self.[16]

Recently, increasing attention has been paid to the situation and status of *intersexuals* as a distinct group falling under the umbrella of "transgenderism." Anne Fausto-Sterling, professor of biology and women's studies at Brown University, writes, "Intersexuality has always been to some extent a matter of definition. And in the past century physicians have been the ones who defined children as intersexual—and provided the remedies."[17] Intersexual persons are certainly a much misunderstood group; their very existence is often considered by some medical professionals to be a type of biological mistake. That opinion is, of course, highly controversial and patently offensive to many intersexual persons. According to Fausto-Sterling:

> The concept of intersexuality is rooted in the very ideas of male and female. In the idealized, Platonic, biological world, human beings are divided into two kinds: a perfectly dimorphic species. Males have an X and a Y chromosome, testes, a penis and all of the appropriate internal plumbing for delivering urine and semen to the outside world. They also have well-known secondary sexual characteristics, including a muscular build and facial hair. Women have two X chromosomes, ovaries, all of the internal plumbing to transport urine and ova to the outside world, a system to support pregnancy and fetal development, as well as a variety of recognizable secondary sexual characteristics.
>
> That idealized story papers over many obvious caveats: some women have facial hair, some men have none; some women speak with deep voices, some men veritably squeak. Less well known is the fact that, on close inspection, absolute dimorphism disintegrates even at the level of basic biology. Chromosomes, hormones, the internal sex structures, the gonads and the external genitalia all vary more than most people realize. Those born outside of the Platonic dimorphic mold are called *intersexuals*.[18]

Physicians have often made arbitrary choices regarding culturally based sexual assignment for intersex persons at birth, including genital surgery and hormone treatments, and this has occasionally led to cognitive dissonance, identity crises, and profound internal anguish for these persons later on during their maturation process. As a result, stories of failed irreversible sexual reassignments within the intersex community have created increased activism on their behalf, and this movement has in turn "led an increasing number of pediatric endocrinologists, urologists and psychologists to reexamine the wisdom of early genital surgery."[19]

In the preceding paragraphs we have very briefly touched upon four types of transgendered persons, each with their own highly distinctive and unique gender-based motivations, needs, and concerns: crossdressers, transgenderists, transexuals, and intersexuals. However, these definitions are actually quite simplistic and do little justice to the many significant variations that exist within the larger transgender community.[20] In truth, there are numerous subdivisions within the various types of transgenderism, each with its own unique elements and manifestations. Though obviously different in many respects, all four types and many other variations as well still fall under the broadly based umbrella category of "transgender."

Differently gendered persons have existed throughout recorded history in all world cultures. Some have been respected and even revered as high-ranking leaders or holy persons. Most, however, seem to have been forced to the margins of their societies.[21]

When we consider the incredible variety that exists within the basic social concept of gender, and even within the highly diverse transgender community itself, it should come as no surprise that there is often much confusion about transgendered persons in the broader culture. One thing is certain: the more we learn about sexual and gender-based variations that exist in nature, the more we realize the ultimate futility of assigning all human beings to a "Platonic dimorphic mode" of identification and expression.

Persons who identify themselves as transgendered usually engage in what may be termed *crossgender* behavior. Transgendered ordained Methodist minister Kathryn J. Helms defines such behavior as assuming the attitudes, role, and dress of the gender role that is opposite to one's biologically determined sex and typical gender role expression. This definition is concise but embraces a spectrum of behavior and attitudes from occasional cross-dressing to transsexual identity. While more typical definitions focus on the "costume" of cross-gender behavior (as witness "cross-dressing") or on sexual identity (as in "transsexual"), the reality is far more complex.

The great ethnologist Clifford Geertz in his book *Local Knowledge* speaks of "thick" definitions and "thin" ones. "Thick" definitions take into account the significance of specified behavior for the person within the culture being studied. "Thin" definitions are external constructs given significance from the culture of the "expert" without tapping the essential self-understanding of those being studied.

Especially in the context of religious behavior the words "cross-dresser" or "transsexual" (and perhaps even "transgendered") become thin, one-dimensional statements, inadequate to define the complexities of cross-gender behavior patterns. It is only when the complexities of these patterns are acknowledged and wrestled with that fair assessments may be made and accurate conclusions drawn.[22]

Typically the religious world has ascribed Geertz's "thin" definitions, or external constructs, to cross-gender behavior and, by association, to those persons who engage in that behavior. Such shallow, "surface" definitions do a grave injustice to the complexities of the lives of transgendered persons.

TRANSGENDERPHOBIA

"Transgenderphobia" refers to the institutionalization and systematizing of prejudice, oppression, and discrimination directed toward persons who are, or who are perceived to be, differently gendered in some way. These attitudes and actions are rooted in a combination of ignorance, misunderstanding, fear, and bigotry.

The current social and systemic normative assumption is that everyone is nontransgendered. This is, quite simply, a premise that cannot stand even the most casual scrutiny. The existence, the experiences, and the considerable daily contributions of differently gendered persons easily prove that assumption wrong. Transgenderphobia needs to be exposed and understood as the unfair, unjust, and corrupt social disease that it is.

Writing on the nature of sin, Rita Nakashima Brock, a leading scholar in the fields of feminist theology and women's studies, writes, "We understand sin as historically and socially produced, which requires us to take responsibility for understanding and stopping sin and oppression."[23] If Brock is correct, then it is indeed the responsibility of each of us to inform ourselves, to learn about the ways in which others are oppressed, i.e., sinned against, and then to fully accept our individual and corporate responsibility for stopping that sin and oppression. A transgender-based liberation theology is necessary so that we may begin effectively articulating the problem, creating solutions, and joining in the ongoing struggle against such oppression.

Many variations of liberation theologies have emerged from oppressed and marginalized communities throughout the world. Such theologies are always contextually rooted in experience—the shared, lived experience of dispossessed and disenfranchised groups. This marginalized experience brings authenticity, depth, richness, insight, challenge, and humanity to the theological dialogue itself. There is a unique but simple power in personal experience that is clearly undeniable. It is rooted in what we know to be true, and we know it is true because we have lived it out and experienced it for ourselves.

4

OPENING PANDORA'S BOX

THERE IS AN ANCIENT MYSTERY involved with being transgendered—the mystery of the social concept of gender and its implications, of transcendent human possibility, and of complex psychoemotional motivations that science and religion have never fully understood. When the circumstances of a differently gendered life are combined with the richness of Christian spirituality we find ourselves confronted with the essence of an even deeper mystery, one that has confounded people throughout the centuries, creating confusion about how one's life fits into God's grand scheme of the universe.

Our process of socialization with its culturally pervasive influences essentially determines our personal and collective paradigm of gender. Gender is primarily a social construct, although we must also recognize the biological component that underlies it. The nature versus nurture argument is one that has long been associated with sex and gender issues (and certainly with gender variant issues). It is inarguably true, however, that our culture has arbitrarily decided what constitutes typical and acceptable behavior and appearance for males and females, and everyone is expected to conform to these culturally determined and enforced gender norms or else face the consequences. Cultures have a broad tendency to "impose system on the inherently untidy experience"[1] of being human and alive.

All people possess certain gender characteristics that are considered to be consistent or inconsistent with their biological sex. Society usually determines or at least heavily

influences our self-concept of gender by teaching us which
gender characteristics should be dominant in our lives. Unfortunately, this social determination is usually based solely
upon the presence of certain physical properties at birth,
i.e., our genitalia—a criterion that should probably be the
least important in determining such an important aspect
of one's existence. As a direct result of these socialization
processes and subsequent cultural expectations, the dominant gender for most people is almost always synonymous
with their physical and anatomical sex. (Whether such a
determination is always healthy or right for them as individuals is quite another matter indeed, as many gender
variant persons can readily attest.) We've already seen that a
certain percentage of the population—the transgendered—
possess a dominant gender that is opposite their physical
and anatomical sex. In the case of intersexual persons,
this socialized gender dynamic may become even more
profoundly complex and potentially confusing.

GENDER ROLES AND THEIR FUNCTIONS

We who are differently gendered perform a critical function for our culture: we challenge society's gender roles and
expectations. We constantly hold gender up for reflection
and assessment, helping to create nuance and meaning even
as we examine and stretch gender's continually evolving,
socially constructed, and highly arbitrary definitions. This
is certainly no small or insignificant cultural task. In her
book *Vested Interests: Cross-dressing and Cultural Anxiety,* Harvard professor and social theorist Marjorie Garber
even goes so far as to suggest that there can be no culture
at all without the transgendered.[2] Whether it recognizes it
or not, the world needs us. Differently gendered persons
serve as sociocultural mirrors, constantly revealing society
to itself and boldly challenging our cognitive and emotional
awareness of what it means to be male, female, or "other"
in this world. Such an awareness inevitably and undeniably

informs society and its sensibilities even as it shapes the actual development of culture, defining and constantly re-defining our enculturated roles as gendered human beings who live and operate within systematic, constructed social contexts.

Context is what gives meaning and structure to the life of any individual or community, and this is true whether that context be personal, cultural, relational, or spiritual. Context is essential for us if we are to understand and cope with our circumstances in this world. Yet, despite the significant role occupied by the gender variant in our society, transgendered Christians have historically been excluded from the central life and spiritual context of the institutional church. The transgendered are a much maligned and unjustly treated group. Regardless of society or the church's attitude toward us, however, God created us as differently gendered people—and because God did so, it means that we are good. Even more, it means that our gender variant lives are holy and our souls are beloved by God.

FEAR AND ITS CONSEQUENCES

J. J. Allen notes,

> As a timeless aspect of the human condition, trans-genderism is truly a Pandora's Box from which spring challenging, complex, and sometimes compellingly unique images and issues: How do we define what it is to be human? How long must it take before we expand the limits of human freedom and expression? How viable are our present concepts of sex, sexuality, and gender?[3]

It is obvious that there are some within our society, and especially within the institutional Christian church as a microcosm of that society, who are frightened practically to the point of hysteria by the diverse and multifaceted social, political, and religious implications of such issues. These

persons would almost certainly obstruct the opening of the
Pandora's Box that is gender, and in their fear would do all
within their power to prevent any direct confrontation with
the questions that the existence of transgendered individuals represents. After all, upsetting the comfort and perceived
security of the social status quo can be a dicey proposition.
It can also mean that we might find ourselves in a place of
discomfort and then have to work our way through it. The
up side is that we are then forced to learn, grow, change our
worldview and behavior, and increase our understanding of
gender and its relevance to our lives.

Opening the forbidden Pandora's Box of gender is indeed
a frightening scenario for many.

> And yet, the very fact that such boxes are forbidden
> is the reason that they must be opened: For those
> boxes contain the great and terrible secrets, experi-
> ences, temptations, and insights we need to uncover
> and explore if we are to fully partake of the mysteries,
> trials, and triumphs of being human.
>
> As God has apparently ordained, there seem to
> be few better at the art of opening forbidden boxes
> than the transgendered. However, that we possess this
> artistry is one reason why we are so often viewed as
> both a fascinating and threatening people.[4]

We are experts at opening those forbidden boxes because
our very lives have been about such mysterious activities.
We're good at it because we *have* to be: our struggles
to recognize and act upon our differently gendered orientation require that we develop artistry and expertise in
opening those boxes. However, lifting the box lid tends
to threaten those who don't understand us. Such persons
can't seem to embrace or even tolerate the mystery, particularly within conservative institutions such as the Christian
church. This perceived threat to socioreligious security,
rooted in a powerful and pervasive paradigm of fear, will
be discussed in greater detail in chapter 10.

RECOGNIZING, DECONSTRUCTING, AND BUILDING

As gender-gifted human beings who are created in the image of God, transgendered people find themselves involved in an ongoing struggle for peace, justice, and personal integrity. After years of living under the culture of silence, some differently gendered persons are beginning to realize that their dehumanizing sociocultural situation is *not* the will of God but a product of social history—and, as a product of social history, that status can be changed.[5] Eleazar Fernandez speaks of this coming to awareness:

> Realizing this dangerous truth, many have gained the courage to bring their long muted anguish into public expression, and they have gained further encouragement upon encountering others on the same journey. Soon each one has realized that she or he is not alone; that there are companions on the long and arduous journey in the struggle for a better society.[6]

There is an incredible worldwide community of amazingly gifted, capable, and compassionate transgendered people who are very willing to affirm and support the struggles and journeys of others like themselves. The World Wide Web is a marvelous tool for differently gendered people to reach out and find groups and individuals. In addition, there are many local transgender social and support organizations across the United States and around the world. "Transgender social networks empower transgendered individuals to free themselves from the control of the medical establishment and establish new forms of relationships and families that support them and their transgendered identities. They create a hospitable niche for transgendered individuals where they can begin to explore the nature of their transgendered lives."[7] We are not alone.

In her book *Gender Outlaw* the delightfully subversive and uniquely talented transgendered author/speaker/playwright/actress/activist Kate Bornstein discusses her reasons for confronting the issue of being differently gendered in an unjust, inflexible, and inequitably gendered society. She tells of a transformational moment, one that serves as a catalyst for action on the gender front:

> Something happens, some final bit that lights up the injustice of the gender system, and in that flash, we see that the emperor is wearing no clothes. That this either/or gender system we've got is truly oppressing us. That happens, and we snap; we begin to fight.... There are a lot of ways to fight, and transgendered people these days are coming together in the common fight for the right to express our genders freely. Where once we met only in drag bars or social teas, we're now meeting at protest marches and in consciousness-raising groups.... We meet to discuss ways and means of securing our freedom. In this struggle for freedom of expression there comes a point where the gender system reveals itself to be not only oppressive, but silly. When we see how ridiculous it is, we can truly begin to dismantle it.[8]

Bornstein's ideas reflect and augment the words of poet, essayist, and activist Audre Lorde, who reminded us that "the master's tools will never dismantle the master's house." In other words, we cannot use the same old oppressive implements of strict, inflexible gender dichotomy to effectively deconstruct and dismantle the dominant and highly restrictive gender system that is currently in place. Instead, we must find new tools—our common sense, our personal and cumulative knowledge and wisdom, our hearts, our minds, our sense of justice, and the leading of the Spirit of God—to bring about the important constructive and transformational changes that are so desperately needed. It won't hurt, either, to be able to chuckle occasionally at a society that insists upon an inflexible system of gender identification based solely upon one's genitalia. Such an impoverished system needs to be transformed so that people can be free to strive toward the amazing possibilities of their human capacity, unimpeded by arbitrary and unfair social gender expectations. Gender liberation isn't only about gender variant people: it's for *everyone*.

Bornstein is right about the need for deconstructing our society's oppressive and confining gender system. She is also right about the necessity for liberating action. I am convinced that differently gendered persons who call ourselves Christian need to begin figuring out how to meet openly in our churches, Bible studies, support groups, and prayer groups as well as at protest marches and gender awareness groups. The spiritual component *must* be an essential, continuous, and core element of our struggle for personal and community justice. Unless we who are gender variant recognize that important truth we will be sorely limited in the effectiveness of our actions toward our own liberation. Any movement that fails to recognize the centrality and the necessity of its spirituality is a movement without a soul, and a soulless movement is ultimately doomed to failure.

Central American, Hispanic, Latino, Latina, *Mujerista*, African-American, and other liberation theologians have known instinctively that we cannot separate the spiritual from the social or the political if we hope to be successful in a liberative struggle. This is why so many priests and nuns as well as other clergy and religious leaders have been active in developing liberation theology movements in various Third World countries. They have understood the necessity for overlapping and synthesizing the spiritual, social, and political spheres in order to work for freedom, justice, and liberation on behalf of God's oppressed people.

ASKING SPIRITUAL QUESTIONS

Spiritual questions are sacred in and of themselves. Those who refuse to take the spiritual questions and concerns of transgendered persons seriously are behaving in direct opposition to God's compassionate invitation for all persons to come into a fulfilling relationship with their Creator. The souls of transgendered people are of as much concern to God as those of any other person and are therefore intrinsically valuable to the Body of Christ.

Christine M. Smith, professor of preaching and worship at United Theological Seminary of the Twin Cities, has written, "To live out of our own integrity as women and men and to base our spirituality and practice of ministry on that integrity demands that we confront and span dichotomies that split, divide, and destroy the world."[9] And who is more aptly suited to spanning and transcending those dichotomies of difference—at least the gender-based differences of dress, appearance, and behavior, with all their profound implications for humankind—than the transgendered, the other, the alien, the stranger in our midst? Who is better equipped than the differently gendered to show us to ourselves, to mirror our gender paradigms, to offer new insights into the mysteries of human ways of being, and to become a strong moral force for good because of those new insights?

Black liberation theologian James Cone writes, "Any interpretation of the Gospel in any historical period that fails to see Jesus as the Liberator of the oppressed is heretical. Any view of the Gospel that fails to understand the Church as that community whose work and consciousness are defined by the community of the oppressed is not Christian and thus heretical."[10] Stephen Breck Reid, professor of Old Testament at Austin Presbyterian Theological Seminary, reinforces Cone's idea: "There is no God but the one of freedom; any deviation from this is heresy."[11] It is historically apparent that the transgendered have and continue to be the victims of socioreligious discrimination, exclusion, marginalization, bigotry, and prejudice, and thus obviously meet any reasonable criteria for inclusion in Cone's "community of the oppressed." If the church fails to play an active part in the liberation process for all the oppressed, including the differently gendered person, then it is acting in a heretical manner that requires transformation at the root.

Becoming a Christian, a believer in the liberating message of Jesus Christ, is a choice that anyone may make at any time. However, it is my opinion, based upon a great deal of research and a lifetime of personal experience, that being authentically gender variant is not really a choice at all. In most cases it seems to be an interesting and highly variegated combination of biology, heredity, and other environmental determinants, none of which are necessarily predicated upon spiritual, moral, or ethical decisions. A unique combination of personal faith and physical reality often creates many layers of spiritual and emotional complexity for Christian persons who lead transgendered lives.

For most differently gendered Christians, the very fact of our existence generally implies a certain degree of struggle in dealing with the essentially sex- and gender-negative, socially determined, and culturally enforced status quo. Oppression in various forms because of our gender status is, quite simply, a given for some of us. In the light of that knowledge, let us attempt to explore the nature of this struggle and its effects on the lives and experiences of persons who, through no fault of their own, are often forced to live on the margins of society and of the church.

ADDRESSING CONCERNS ABOUT TRANSGENDERISM

S OME WHO READ THESE WORDS will be unfamiliar with the concept or the experience of being differently gendered in a male-female polarized, sex- and gender-negative culture. Nevertheless, I hope that your innate sense of justice and fairness will allow you to suspend whatever culturally instilled inhibitions, biases, or unfounded negativity you may initially harbor toward these issues.

We are talking about the real lives of real people who are living in the real world and dealing with real concerns. These people and their issues are not to be dismissed as irrelevant or trivial.

We are *not* transgendered because we are under a curse, as some have believed at various times and for various reasons. Being differently gendered is a curse only if we believe it to be so. *All* people are beautiful and beloved in the sight of God, for we are created in God's own image. And if we are created in God's image then God is somehow not complete without each of us. Some people perceive a transgendered orientation as a curse because they have been socialized and culturally conditioned to believe that. Differently gendered folks (along with the rest of society) are taught to think that way so that those in positions of social and institutional dominance can maintain their positions of power and authority by using the transgendered as convenient scapegoats. They make us feel inferior, planting the seeds of doubt and fear while keeping us confused and taking advantage of our relatively powerless social, political, and spiritual situation. It may perhaps be difficult for some nontransgendered persons to accept, but the lives of differently gendered people can be as profound and have as much to offer the church as those of any other group or individuals.

Who are the transgendered Christians and where do we find them? Differently gendered Christians are human beings very much like everyone else, with spiritual, emotional, and physical needs and concerns just like everyone else, who laugh and cry and eat and drink and fall in love and go to work and pay bills and have families and strengths and weaknesses just like everyone else, and who deserve to live their lives and be treated with dignity, respect, and acceptance just like everyone else.

Transgendered people are everywhere, in all walks of life and in all segments of society. In addition, gender variant persons have a long and storied history. We were known to Hippocrates and Herodotus in ancient Greece, and we were around in the Middle East during the time of the writings of the Hebrew scriptures. However, much of transgendered history has been hidden or obscured by the powers that be in attempts to discredit or trivialize the contributions of gender variant people to society.[1] Transgendered people have lived on the margins of society even though we have been and continue to be present in every culture across the globe. Although the attitude of negativity may have been ameliorated in some quarters (particularly among the many people who are learning that transgendered persons are, in truth, their beloved family members, friends, neighbors, coworkers, teachers, pastors, church members, and fellow citizens), the fact is that the differently gendered are still mainly looked upon as outsiders, interlopers, threats, and gender outlaws by our cultural and institutional gatekeepers.

Gender variant persons must continually deal with the cultural assumption that we are somehow intrinsically flawed or disordered. "Demonstrating gender traits or identity that challenge expectations inevitably evokes the reaction that something is wrong with us."[2] Most people are ill equipped and uninformed about how to deal with someone who is differently gendered. They have little or no accurate knowledge about the lives and needs of transgendered individuals, and they just don't know what to do with us.

CONCERNING TRANSGENDERED CHILDREN

Our society rather naïvely tends to regard producing a differently gendered child as an occurrence somewhat more rare than being abducted by extraterrestrials, so it should not surprise us that most people are simply unprepared to deal with the eventuality of a transgendered person in their lives. This is why some transgendered children "who are forced to comply with social stereotypes may develop behavioral problems, which may lead to depression and other serious mental health issues, caused not by the gender variant nature, but by society's non-acceptance of them."[3] Transgendered children know about bullies, too. They quickly learn that bullies have a specific social function: they define the limits of acceptable conduct, appearance, and activities for children. They enforce rigid expectations. They are masters of the art of humiliation and technicians of the science of terrorism. Differently gendered kids usually have nowhere to turn for help when confronted by the bullies of our culture. "There are virtually no social supports in any of our social services or educational institutions for a child who is gender variant."[4] There's absolutely nothing available for transgendered youth or adults in most of the Christian church, either. If hurting, confused transgendered children cannot turn to their community of faith without fear of being judged or shunned, where can they turn?

As we've already seen, our traditional institutions (the church, the military, the educational system, business, industry, etc.) usually consider the transgendered to be "problem people," some sort of pernicious threat to Western civilization as we know it. But differently gendered individuals are not "problem people" at all. We are a people with problems, most of them created by the very society that ignorantly, irrationally, and arbitrarily condemns and oppresses us for no reason other than the fact that we're benignly "different" in our appearance and gender-based behavior.

Leslie Feinberg, outspoken female-to-male transgender activist, writes tellingly of the childhood pain of growing up differently:

> I didn't want to be different. I longed to be everything grownups wanted, so they would love me. I followed their rules, tried my best to please. But there was something about me that made them knit their eyebrows and frown. No one ever offered me a name for what was wrong with me. That's what made me afraid it was really bad. I only came to recognize its melody through its constant refrain: "Is it a boy or girl?"
>
> "I'm sick of people asking me if she's a boy or a girl," I overheard my mother complain to my father. "Everywhere I take her, people ask me."
>
> I was ten years old. I was no longer a little kid and I didn't have a sliver of cuteness to hide behind. The world's patience with me was fraying, and it panicked me. When I was really small I thought I would do anything to change whatever was wrong with me. Now I didn't want to change. I just wanted people to stop being mad all the time.[5]

THE SIGNIFICANCE OF IGNORANCE AND NEGATIVITY

People are often afraid of what they don't understand. Ignorance can lead to fear, fear to anger, and anger to various

forms of oppression. Unfortunately, such misunderstand-
ings are often directed toward those who are different,
whether that difference is racial, sexual, religious, gender
based, or other, and that is why minorities are the targets
of so many types of discrimination. Gamson states:

> Most people's personal identities, and many people's
> social and political identities, depend on clear, binary
> categories; they depend on an assumption that the
> difference between groups is hard, fast, and recogniz-
> able. Power and privilege also ride the classifications.
> In political systems such as this one that distribute
> power, rights and resources along gender lines, there
> is certainly a logic to guarding the clarity of those
> boundaries.[6]

The fact that gender variant persons blur or transgress those
boundaries is the reason for the existence of so much socialized antipathy and hostility toward us. It's also the reason
why differently gendered people deserve legal protection
from discrimination and oppression, certainly as much as
any other minority group that needs protection by law.
Transgendered persons are among those groups that are
told by society and its institutions, including the church,
"We wish you were invisible; we don't accept you. We
wish you would simply go away, and we will pretend that
you don't exist. We will ostracize and marginalize you. We
will deny you any rights because you are different and we
hate you."

Some differently gendered people admittedly suffer from
self-destructive behaviors and low self-esteem. Rates of drug
abuse, alcoholism, depression, self-mutilation, and suicide
within the gender variant community are several times the
national average. However, difficulties such as these are
not created by the existence of a transgender orientation in
and of itself. For the most part, these very real problems
are the inevitable result of being raised in dysfunctional
circumstances within a culture that is transgenderphobic

and overtly hostile toward those who are "different." To illustrate this point, transgendered social activist Riki Anne Wilchins tells us very bluntly,

> Trans-identity is not a natural fact. Rather, it is the political category we are forced to occupy when we do certain things with our bodies. That so many of us try to take our own lives, mutilate ourselves, or just succeed in dying quietly of shame, depression, or loneliness is not an accident. We are supposed to feel isolated and desperate. That is the whole point of the system. Our feelings are not causes but effects.[7]

Wilchins powerfully reminds us that many of our differently gendered sisters and brothers are living lives of desperation and distress, often through no fault of their own.

Adding to this climate of negativity is the unpleasant reality that some people in positions of power seem to be much more interested in maintaining their version of "order," via rigid enforcement of the institutional status quo, than they are in actively seeking justice and liberation for those who need it most. In other words, the institution's perceived needs are always supposed to come before those of the individual.[8]

Our culture's institutions, however, are ultimately composed of human individuals, and therefore the civil rights and human needs of every person ought to be considered at least as important as, if not more important than, those of the institutions themselves. In theory, influential social institutions such as government or the Christian church should exist to be the tool or the servant of the people, not the other way around. At the very moment when a compassionate focus on the rights of the individual is lost, the foundations of the institution—and thus, by extension, of society itself—paradoxically also begin to crumble. It is in society's own best interests to actively promote and guard the well-being, rights, and freedom of the individual so it can more effectively preserve and maintain the structural integrity of our worthwhile institutions and even of society itself.

PREVAILING SOCIORELIGIOUS ATTITUDES TOWARD THE TRANSGENDERED

Those who fear, hate, discriminate against, and exclude the transgendered (or any other oppressed minority groups) often appear to be the routine and even rather predictable products of their culture. Vitriolic attitudes toward the differently gendered are the almost inevitable result of a long-term and pervasive religio-cultural ideology that teaches that it's perfectly permissible and even virtuous to think, speak, and act in a destructive or vicious manner toward other human beings who are different in some way. The need to dominate and oppress others is primarily based on psychoemotional pain. This is how childhood (and adult) bullies are created; mentally healthy people don't need to dominate and oppress others. Persons engaging in such behaviors are acting out by misdirecting their internal anguish and antagonism toward the gender variant, not toward the real source of their pain. That source of pain is, at least in part, the unjust and harmful prevailing social paradigm of gender and its unjust expectations, an archetype that essentially forces human beings into straitjacketed, rigid, and inflexible gender roles and characterizations, resulting in warped, distorted versions of human relationships and treatment.

The transgendered have traditionally been targeted as socially acceptable scapegoats, and some individuals and groups unfortunately have a strong penchant for taking advantage of that culturally condoned opportunity. Thus, we see what is really happening with regard to our society's treatment of the differently gendered: it has to do with the dynamics and the political maneuverings of power at work. Our society is structured so that one group will always maintain power over another through strict adherence to and enforcement of designated cultural mores. Transformational strategies such as the struggle for liberative justice are necessary to change that objectionable, destructive situation for the betterment of all. But transformational efforts and change agents are always resisted by persons and institutions in power—especially the ones who have the most power to lose and who are therefore the most threatened—and so the struggle between these opposing factions is intense and ongoing.

As John Shelby Spong reminds us, however, "When issues are being fought over in a changing world, those who risk rejection by embracing the future and moving beyond the barriers of past prejudices are never finally hurt. Those who cling to the insights of a dying world or a passing prejudice are the ones who will ultimately lose both credibility and integrity."[9]

THE TRANSGENDERED AND THE CHURCH

Given the stark reality of this power-based social structure, we might ask ourselves, "Why should transgendered people care at all about the Christian church, an institution that continually seems to reinforce our marginalized status and is definitely not in favor of having us around? Why do we bother to stay in the church, especially when those in positions of power would much rather see us go away and stop embarrassing or inconveniencing them by our very presence? Why should we want to cling to an outmoded religious institution that changes so slowly and treats members of its own constituency so unjustly and oppressively? Why do we have such strong spiritual, emotional and psychological ties to this institution, a church that has so wounded us?" These are important questions. A large part of the answer is simply that the church is our spiritual heritage; it's an irreplaceable part of who and what we are as spiritual persons. Therefore, we cannot easily dismiss it or walk away from it, even though some are eventually and painfully forced to do so.

Personally, I find myself loving the immense potential of the church much more than the reality that the institutional church currently embodies. The Christian church's possibilities are incredibly exciting to me, and opportunity exists for the institution to be a wonderfully effective agency for great good. However, the present sad reality is that the forces of religion, particularly the more conservative, fundamentalist segments of Christianity, are actively aligned against any person or group appearing to threaten its pervasive system of patriarchy, androcentrism, sexism, misogyny, homophobia, heterosexism, transgenderphobia, and male-dominated hierarchy. This is not to say that good cannot or does not come from the church currently, nor do I mean to imply in any way that godly, compassionate people do not exist or function actively within the church's religious system. But much of the good that the church generates is far too often undermined by a power-based and elitist religious attitude that permeates the church's infrastructure to its core. The Christian church's vested interest in the perpetuation of an oppressive status quo renders it highly unlikely that a genuine spiritual awakening and transformation based upon a Christlike attitude of compassion and justice for the disenfranchised will occur inside this institution without a great deal of political difficulty and ongoing struggle. Amos 5:24 says, "Let justice roll down like waters, and righteousness like a neverending stream," but, for the differently gendered and other oppressed peoples in the church, justice usually tends to roll down more like molasses.

Once people have been labeled as outcasts or have been stigmatized by the church because of who or what they are, they are going to have a great deal of trouble hearing and responding to the good news of the Gospel. Why should people even care to listen to the good news of Jesus Christ if they are being censured, ostracized, or otherwise oppressed by the same church that ostensibly preaches the love of God out of the other side of its mouth? Is Christ's love indeed meant for *all* people, or is it not? Is that divine grace extended in complete, total inclusivity to all human beings, or is it not? Are the church's promises at our baptism—to welcome us, love us, and pray for us—legitimate, or are those promises simply hollow, conditional rhetoric, extended only to those who meet arbitrary, socially constructed, gender- or sexually based criteria? These may appear to be simplistic, rhetorical questions at first glance, but I don't recall Jesus ever attempting any sort of qualifying procedure in deciding to whom he would minister. Jesus set the example for us: he never refused to love or accept *anyone* who came to him with a genuine desire to experience God's presence and truth. He never told people to go away and not bother him until they could find some way to be more socially acceptable (e.g., the thief on the cross, Luke 23:39–43).

Those who are starving will not be overly moved to listen to a sermon filled with pious religious platitudes until they are fed, and those who are physically sick will probably not be prepared to hear about Jesus until they are well enough to do so. Similarly, those who are being treated unjustly will not be highly motivated to hear the good news proclaimed by those who purportedly represent Jesus while at the same time excluding the very people who desire to be accepted.

People must be met, loved, served, and ministered to at their point of greatest need. Only then can the truth of the Gospel be effective and meaningful for them; they will have seen and experienced Christ's love in action for themselves, expressed and embodied through specific acts of justice and compassion. The essence of the Gospel is to bring the good news of liberation, salvation, and redemption to the poor, the outcast, the suffering, and the oppressed.

REMAINING WITHIN THE CHURCH

This, then, is why I stay in the church, as difficult as that decision sometimes becomes: because God has called me to remain within the Body of Christ, working for transformation even as I attempt to serve others in the name of the One who created us in love and for love. The compelling need for the development of a specifically transgender-based liberation theology becomes even more evident when considered from this perspective of holy inclusivity. The Gospel was freely given to *all* people and, even more specifically, to those whom our religious traditions have told us to exclude and reject. Differently gendered people need spiritual ministry just like everyone else, and Christians can begin that ministry by extending hope, acceptance, respect, dignity, and mutuality in Jesus' name to the gender variant who seek a relationship with God and with God's church.

Jesus is to be our role model both in service and in the struggle for justice. Of course, we must remember that the socioreligious authorities of his day eventually killed him for his outspoken activism on the part of the disempowered and disenfranchised. Such are the ramifications of caring about, expressing concern for, and taking action on behalf of the community of the oppressed. It's dangerous and sometimes fatal to become involved with those whom the establishment rejects. Beverly Harrison, feminist theologian and professor of Christian ethics at Union Theological Seminary, writes of the deadly social dynamic involved in the crucifixion of Christ: "Jesus' death on a cross, his sacrifice, was no abstract exercise in moral virtue. His death was the price he paid for refusing to abandon the radical activity of love—of expressing solidarity and reciprocity with the excluded ones in his community."[10]

Jesus continually spoke out against the hypocrisy of distorted, warped religion and its power-hungry leaders. He always emphasized the importance of a personal, spirit-filled relationship with God over that of fanatical devotion to dogmatic tradition and ostentatious religious piety. He lovingly demonstrated how to live and how to relate to our Creator and to each other. But through the example of Jesus we also learn that there is always a sobering price to pay for attempting to transform the entrenched system and the status quo. Those in positions of power seldom give up their power without a struggle, and so we must boldly and prayerfully enter that struggle ourselves if we are to make a legitimate difference in changing the oppressive system.

Christ calls each of us to share the Gospel in love through the conscious act of creating justice and freedom for all people in this world. As we strive to bring about that justice, we may also help to create a new climate of liberative spiritual freedom. Such freedom can subsequently allow us to know God, each other, and ourselves in new, dynamic, and glorious ways that will further enhance and fulfill our lives as we operate in the service of Jesus Christ. I stay within the church because I desperately want to see justice and love win; I want to see us *all* win.

6

"COMPASSIONATE CONDEMNATION"

THIS CHAPTER IS PAINFUL for me to write, and I am sure it will be painful for many to read. I apologize in advance for that and wish it weren't necessary, but, unfortunately, oppressive attitudes and actions on the part of some within the Body of Christ make it so. The following accounts by differently gendered persons who have found themselves in conflict with the church are taken directly from personal correspondence or conversations that I have had over the last few years. My reason for including these stories is to give readers a brief idea of how the real lives of some transgendered persons are being damaged and trampled upon by the church, an institution that is supposed to reflect the loving, highly inclusive character of Jesus but that in reality often refuses to recognize or accept the diversity, the goodness, and the many spiritual contributions that the gender variant have to offer.

Most mainstream denominations have set up task forces, committees, or other groups to "study" the situation regarding sexual minorities. This is at least a start, and it perhaps shows good intentions, but it is nowhere near enough. The churches have not yet begun "studying" *gender* minorities. The problem with study groups of this kind is that while they spend time—sometimes decades—"analyzing the problem," devising "approaches" and various "methodologies," and often "tabling the discussion for further research," transgendered people are left to twist in the wind, remaining outside of what should be the institutional church's welcoming embrace. "Continued 'conversation' does not serve those who are disenfranchised."[1]

I am a Christian who loves and supports the church of Jesus Christ, and it is not my intention to bash the Christian community, to destroy it, or to malign it unfairly. It *is* my purpose, however, to inform readers by increasing awareness of what's going on in the lives of transgendered people as they interact with the church in various situations and capacities. Some persons and organizations on the religious right have used the phrase "compassionate condemnation" as a convenient euphemism for their oppressive attitudes and actions toward any person or behavior that they consider to be sinful or religiously unacceptable. Christian people of conscience can no longer afford or allow the extreme religious right to define or police Christianity to the exclusion of those who are "different" in some way. Too many are being hurt as a result of those extremist tactics; even one person is too many. It is incumbent upon the Body of Christ to welcome, affirm, validate, respect, and love the transgendered individual just as God does and always has.

I wish I could say that the personal accounts that follow are exceptions, that such situations rarely occur, and that most of the time the institutional church deals fairly and respectfully with transgendered people. Unfortunately, this is simply not the case. Most mainline Christian denominations reject and condemn transgendered appearance, behavior, and orientation out of hand. I once saw a transgendered person wearing a T-shirt that bore the message: "Jesus hates me, this I know, for the Christians tell me so."

MISGUIDED ASSUMPTIONS

In some circles, all transgendered people are assumed to be gay or lesbian. However, such a supposition is highly incorrect, and our society needs to learn that the transgender community is much more complex than this blanket

presumption might indicate. While I fully support and promote the inclusion of gay, lesbian, and bisexual persons in
all areas of the life of the church, including the ordained
clergy, it's a fact that sexual orientation and gender orientation are essentially two very different (though occasionally
overlapping) human phenomena. Documented research on
file with the International Foundation for Gender Education
indicates that most differently gendered people appear to
be, in fact, heterosexually oriented. Blindly lumping sexual
and gender orientation together illustrates either vindictive-
ness or wholesale ignorance on the part of those who would
use the "homosexuality argument" to condemn all gender
variant persons.

Many within the Christian church base their disapproval
of differently gendered persons upon a particular, yet extremely narrow and often ill-informed, hermeneutic. It is
true, I will freely admit, that the Bible (at least when
literally interpreted) does not appear to lend the transgendered much sympathy. This is because, for most people,
the Bible's interpretation is largely determined by the ubiquitous, gender-specific cultural mores that have dominated
our conservative socioreligious history for the past several centuries. No matter how honest or unbiased we may
wish to be in interpreting scripture, we almost always
make our hermeneutical determinations within the context of the cultural conditioning and social expectations
in which we have been raised. In terms of attitudes and
opinions about transgendered persons, most of us already
possess a predetermined inclination, one that inevitably influences our theology, our interpretation of scripture, and
our worldview.

Rather than trying to engage the scriptures without pre-
condition or bias, many people begin with a culturally
derived sense that such "perversity" or "deviance," i.e., gender variant dress or behavior, is plainly wrong and sinful in
the eyes of God. (They usually can't tell you exactly why
that should be so, but they're certain that it is. After all,

the Bible must condemn such behavior somewhere!) Such a mindset is the almost inevitable product of an institutional, patriarchal Christian belief system that considers itself authoritative in scriptural interpretation and that is not passive in its pursuit of a commonality in thought and behavior for all "true believers." This system often reflects a religiously based desire to find "*the* truth," a "truth" that will always apply equally to everyone everywhere, regardless of circumstance or personal orientation. However, such single-minded formulas rigidly condemn or dismiss anyone who disagrees with them and never take into account the divinely created variance of human nature and experience.

Convinced that God could never countenance any views other than those they espouse (and brandishing their King James Bibles, dogmatic slogans, and highly selective codes of imposed morality like machetes while muttering occasional oaths about "smiting the Sodomites"), the self-appointed defenders of religious legalism, conformist behavior, and biblical literalism eagerly gird themselves with the "armor of God" and "march into battle for Jesus" against the "degenerates." Transgendered Christians have often become the unwilling victims of such religious bigotry and attack, as we shall discover in the following vignettes. As Carter Heyward reminds us, "There are many ways to live as fully human beings in God. Religious self-righteousness is not one of them."[2]

CYNTHIA'S STORY

Our first account is from a transgendered Christian whom we'll call Cynthia.[3] She writes:

About five years ago I felt the desire to honestly disclose my transgendered self to my wife and pastor. Upon doing so, I was humiliated and treated as though I had confessed to child molesting. The assumption was that I must be gay even if I insisted I was not. My wife was counseled to leave me. In retrospect, I think she might be better off now if she had. Anyhow, all sorts of negative and totally inappropriate stereotypes were applied to me.

I was sent to a Christian counselor that "specialized" in this sort of thing. He told me that my transgendered behavior was borderline insanity. He probably would have diagnosed me as insane, but he didn't in order to allow me to continue functioning in society. This was done more for his convenience and that of the church than for me. After all, if I lost my job because of this, then who would pay the counselor and make those weekly donations to the church? To tell the truth, I somehow wanted to believe he was right in his assessment, but deep inside I knew his allegations just weren't true. I felt really bad about myself and the mess I was in, but I just couldn't make myself believe that I was close to insanity.

After extensive "therapy," the counselor pronounced me "delivered, set free, etc." We left that church because I couldn't face the pastor or his wife, plus I was not trusted to be alone with children! My own children have no knowledge of any of this, but I do spend a great deal of time talking with them about the gift of God's unconditional love and how that's the most important thing a Christian should demonstrate toward others.

Sometimes the whole thing almost makes me laugh (I have an admittedly strange sense of humor, and it's probably better to laugh about this than cry all the time). It's almost like an episode of "The Three Stooges Exorcise Cynthia's Demon": "Hey, Moe, hand me that cross so I can beat her over the head with it. Then let's bring in the Bible-thumping psychiatrist to finish her off! Woo, woo woo!" With attitudes like those, I can certainly understand why many of our transgendered people leave the church completely.

Cynthia's story is a prime example of the insidious nature of toxic religion. In and of itself, being transgendered has nothing to do with being insane or mentally unstable. If insanity or other symptoms of mental illness should occur in the life of a transgendered individual it is usually because society has created undue stress and difficulty for that person, and the presence of these health problems is often a very natural response to the unfounded negativity and disapproval that our society continues to direct toward the gender variant.

Cynthia's story illustrates one of the ways in which mainstream religion continues to foster an attitude of ignorance regarding a transgender orientation. One cannot—and, indeed, should not—be "delivered" or "set free" from something that is a God-given, holy, and gifted aspect of one's personality. "Ex-gay/lesbian/bisexual/transgender" ministries (and I use the term "ministries" very loosely) do more harm to the cause of Christ than almost any other agencies that fall under the auspices of the Christian church. Such groups and organizations demonically perpetuate the myth of actually being able to "change" through prayer and the denial of a God-given orientation. You may be able to choose your behavior, but if you are oriented toward being transgendered and don't act benignly upon that orientation then you will almost surely pay a heavy psychological, emotional, physical, and spiritual price at some point. *There are no legitimately "ex-transgendered" Christians.* There are only unfortunate souls who: (1) were never genuinely transgendered in the first place, or (2) are either confused or misguided, perhaps by their religion or its leaders, or (3) are being fooled into thinking they're following God's will by repressing a core aspect of themselves.

If people tell you that they can truly deny, walk away from, or "pray away" a genuine transgendered psycho-emotional orientation, then it's probably safe to say that they're lying, are deceived, or were never really differently gendered in the first place. You may change how you behave, but you can't—and have no legitimate reason to—change a God-given, blessed gender variant orientation.

Attempting to do so is an insult to the very God who created us as transgendered.

Cynthia's experience with her church was, unfortunately, not at all rare or unusual. Such injustices are often a fact of life for gender variant Christians. It saddens and angers me that the Christian church should be so hostile and negative toward people simply because they are different, especially when that "difference" is totally benign and harms no one.

I cannot overstate the damage that has been done through the persistent perpetuation of the myth that transgendered people, gays, lesbians, and bisexuals are child molesters. This pernicious, wickedly destructive stereotype has been proven patently false by study after study. Many of the gender and sexually variant people whom I know are parents who adore their children; they would rather die than harm a child. All reputable research has inarguably shown that the overwhelming majority of people who molest children are heterosexual, nontransgendered, and usually persons known to the child.

TRACY'S STORY

Another example of the institutional church's antipathy toward transgendered Christians is found in Tracy's account:

I was "outed" to my pastor and his associates by some well-intentioned friends. This was several years ago at the church I had attended since 1978, and where I grew up spiritually. It is a charismatic word/faith church of about eight hundred people. I had been actively and visibly involved with their rather prominent praise and worship team for eleven years when this "outing" occurred. My marriage of six years at that time was troubled, and most people in our church were aware that we were having problems. My wife knew a bit of my interest in crossdressing and was totally opposed to it.

As I grew older, the need to explore and express my feminine desires became overpowering. In my desperation for knowledge, experiences, and acceptance, I tried to reach out to other Christians for friendship and support. I had what I thought were some private, confidential conversations with a few friends who were all connected with my church in some way. I naïvely came out to these people, thinking I was finding loving Christian supporters. I was wrong.

These people began gossiping among themselves and comparing notes on me, and then they went to our pastor. I was called in to meet with him and his associate and was confronted about the conversations. They asked me to come clean to them, and I did. Their idea was that I should confess my sin of crossdressing, all of it, then repent from it and vow never to engage in any crossdressing activity again. They opted not to tell my wife, as they were aware that things were not that great at home and this news wouldn't help the relationship.

They insisted that I step down from my position in the music ministry. They wouldn't tell the congregation why, but would simply say it was for personal reasons. I was a trusted long-time church member, and they prayed with me asking God to deliver me from this temptation.

Several weeks later, I was asked to come to meet with the associate pastor one evening in his office. We engaged in idle small talk with no apparent agenda, and I wondered aloud why I was asked to come in. The associate pastor's wife entered the office at this point and asked us to come to the conference room. When we did, I was shocked to find my wife, the church staff, and the people with whom I'd had those conversations seated there. Each one told their story about what I had said to them. My wife was hearing all this for the first time. Somehow, they all thought that I hadn't discontinued this activity. Apparently, this idea came from something one of them had said, and this was their method of intervention.

The pastor questioned me about my sexuality. He asked me if I had sexually abused my young son.[4] I had a history of financial struggles and they figured it was probably a result of my "hidden sins." To make a long story short, I was forced to apologize and repent before all of these people. It was a miserable night. My wife was demolished, and I was totally humiliated. They required me to submit to weekly counseling regarding my family finances and my sexual "problem." I went along with their plan, and once a week for a few months I met with a lay member who meant well but had no clue how to deal with me.

Within a few months, I left that church never to return. All this was six or seven years ago. My marriage never got on a good track after that; my wife separated from me earlier this year and is now filing for divorce. I don't know if we could have made our marriage work or not, but the stress and pressure from that church made reconciliation between us impossible. My crossdressing wasn't even a primary cause of the separation, but the church seemed to think that it was. I don't blame God for all this, but I sure do have some problems with pastors and churches who think they have the right to sit in judgment on the rest of us.

Once more I want to emphasize that one cannot "pray away" a genuine transgender orientation—it's an impossibility. Despite the claims of certain "faith healing" charlatans, God doesn't work that way and never has. God certainly can and does heal sickness when God chooses to do so, but there is no reason for God or anyone else to cure someone of being differently gendered: it's not a disease, so why cure it? An individual may decide to repress or deny a legitimate internal differently gendered orientation but will almost surely suffer psychologically, emotionally, spiritually, and physically if that person chooses such an inevitably harmful, self-imposed path. There is, however, absolutely no choice involved with regard to a transgender orientation in a person's life; it either exists or it doesn't, and the individual has no control over that existence whatsoever. You don't choose to be transgendered: a gender variant orientation chooses you, according to God's divine plan for your

life. The only control that may realistically be exercised lies
in the area of specific behaviors, never that of an internal
orientation.

It is disgraceful that "Christian" people should be so
untrustworthy in terms of maintaining confidentiality, but
that's exactly what occurred in this instance. Tracy apparently made a mistake in trusting the other church members
to keep the confidences she shared with them. Perhaps if
Tracy's wife had been willing to deal with Tracy's crossdressing within the context of their marriage then Tracy
wouldn't have felt such an overwhelming need to go to
other people for support and affirmation. (Feelings of loneliness and isolation can be powerful motivations, as many
transgendered persons are acutely aware.) I don't necessarily condone Tracy's actions in this regard, although I can
certainly understand her desire for friendship and valida-
tion from others during a troubled time in her life. We all
need help and acceptance sometimes; the need for support
and affirmation from others is a strong one, particularly for
those who are living with a complex "secret" like Tracy's.
In hindsight, she would probably have been much better off
seeking out a professional therapist or an informed pastoral
counselor. To her credit, Tracy "came clean" about her lack
of discretion and accepted her own responsibility in this situation. The rest of the blame in this story must lie with
those judgmental "Christians" who appointed themselves
the moral judges over a long-time church member who was
apparently a well-respected member of the ministry team.

Was it wrong for Tracy to crossdress? Certainly not. Who
was harmed by it? Was it wrong to express and experience her differently gendered self? No, of course not. That
transgender component was a gift from God, and a healthy,
respectful expression of such a gender-gift is never wrong.
Was it wrong to want to reach out to others for valida-
tion and support? That's difficult to say, but at least some
of her desired emotional and spiritual support should probably have been available from her spouse. However, Tracy's

wife was apparently too caught up in a traditional socio-religious mindset that didn't allow for any sort of flexibility or variation when it came to gender expression. If that supposition is true then Tracy's wife must assume at least some of the responsibility.

Unnecessarily tragic situations result when the church refuses to follow Christ's example of love, liberation, acceptance, inclusivity, and respect for the benign differences and variations that exist within humankind. I am *not* saying that anything goes, nor that we should do away with all standards for ethics, morality, and behavior. I'm simply trying to make the point that dogmatic religious rigidity at the expense of someone's sense of self-worth and self-esteem is a dangerous and unholy thing to perpetrate upon another human being. Holding everyone to an arbitrary standard of sameness as it pertains to gender orientation and related behavior is unrealistic, unnatural, spiritually irresponsible, and certainly anti-diversity (and thus in direct opposition to all of God's diverse creation). In short, it is idolatrous and heretical to make gender-based social mores or expectations more important than the well-being of a person made in God's image.

If Tracy had felt free to be her transgendered Christian self and to express that self openly with the love and support of her wife, it is entirely possible that none of these unfortunate events would have occurred. There would probably have been little or no need for Tracy to go outside her marriage relationship to seek out a primary source of acceptance and support. Also, and irrespective of the attitude of Tracy's spouse toward the crossdressing, the other church members certainly could have been more loving and respectful of Tracy's human dignity. Treating Tracy like a pervert or a suspected criminal served no long-term purpose other than to alienate and deeply wound a loyal church member. No one should have to suffer the sort of harassment and public humiliation that Tracy did, especially at the hands of so-called Christians. Even in a secular court of law one is considered to be innocent until proven guilty. Tracy's church leadership wouldn't even adhere to that minimal standard. The church drove away a highly effective and contributing member of the praise and worship ministry team. Everyone lost. The church's ministry was compromised, relationships were destroyed, and it didn't have to be that way.

PHILIP'S STORY

Philip is a female-to-male transsexual in his mid-forties. His journey toward self-acceptance and understanding has not been without its struggles, particularly in the area of spirituality:

I believe I knew from very early on that something didn't fit in my life, and that gender had something to do with it. Dolls, jump rope, tea parties, girl things in general were by turns meaningless and baffling to me. I was drawn as a child to cars, baseball, the military, and other interests which were socially defined as boy things, but I had no way to pursue these interests in the gender-segregated time and place where I grew up. I coped by reading a lot, by being good at school, and by being quiet. (Two of the three have served me well, but I'm seriously reexamining being quiet.)

I have simply never felt a good fit between who I am inside—my heart, mind, and spirit—and the female gender that I was assigned at birth based on that cursory inspection that all newborns get. I have tried, more or less at any given moment in my life, to find a way to fit by hunching this way and stretching the other way. But after forty-five years of hunching and crunching and stretching to give the illusion of fitting, the fit is no better than it ever was, and the pain can be overwhelming.

In 1997–98 I belonged to the Presbyterian Church and was attending seminary. My plan was to graduate and go into pastoral ministry, hoping and praying that Presbyteri-

ans would soon begin accepting openly GLBT (gay, lesbian, bisexual, and transgendered) persons as pastoral candidates. I was working with a local congregation as a part of my seminary field education (i.e., my internship). During that time the Presbyterian Church USA was struggling with the issue of gay, lesbian, bisexual, and transgender inclusion, and an article called Amendment A was voted on during the national assembly of the denomination. Amendment A was the "inclusion" amendment, and its passage would mean that the Presbyterian Church had become more enlightened and accepting of its GLBT members and clergy. However, the amendment was defeated, mostly through the efforts of a right-wing, conservative faction.

By a strange twist of fate, I was scheduled to preach the following Sunday. I had planned to preach on liberation and thanksgiving, hoping and even presuming that Amendment A would pass. However, I became so discouraged by the outcome of the national assembly's vote against Amendment A that I found I could no longer, in good conscience, continue to belong to a faith community that chose to exclude some of its members from full participation. I was overcome with grief, sadness, frustration, and anger at the church's unwillingness to accept otherwise qualified ministerial candidates, and so I left the Presbyterian Church altogether. I couldn't serve there. It just didn't feel like home to me anymore.

Philip's emotional and spiritual response to the church's negativity toward GLBT persons is certainly understandable. Here was an intelligent, willing, gender variant student of theology who wanted only to be accepted and allowed to faithfully serve the church in a pastoral capacity. However, the forces of bigotry and prejudice worked to prevent that, causing Philip to decide to leave the church altogether—and once again, everyone lost. Philip lost an opportunity to become an effective ordained minister, and the church lost a very capable servant. It didn't have to be that way.

RITA'S STORY

I am often reminded forcefully of the damage that is done to transgendered persons by an inflexible, unyielding religious belief system that allows no room for variation or human difference. The following account is adapted from a letter written by Rita, a married male-to-female crossdresser with children, who is overwhelmed by her religious turmoil with regard to her gender status. As we will discover, Rita's internal transgendered reality is in serious conflict with the negative messages that her religious beliefs impose upon her. Rita is trapped by a religion that collides head-on with her personal experience and legitimate human need:

I am a fifty-year-old male-to-female crossdresser who lives in a northern tier city. I have suppressed my crossdressing tendencies for forty years because as a Christian I believe that such behavior is wrong. Nevertheless, I "came out" as a crossdresser to my family last fall and have since separated from my wife, my children, and my church. It's sad for me to say it, but crossdressing was the only thing in my life that allowed me to experience some genuine moments of peace in my life. However, I went through a purge[5] last December and tried to "go straight" with the help of a counselor. It didn't work. It only caused me to cry just to think that I could never wear women's clothes again.

I have been an evangelical Pentecostal Christian since I was seven years old. I still believe with all my heart that Jesus died for my sins, but I am having great difficulty merging my crossdressing needs with my Christian beliefs. I feel like I am rebelling against God. I think it is mostly due to God's condemnation of crossdressing in Deuteronomy 22:5, where it says, "A woman shall not wear anything that pertains to a man, nor shall a man put on a woman's garment, for all that do so are an abomination to the Lord your God."

This verse is the one that caused me to suppress my cross-dressing tendencies all of my Christian life. I have sought God for over forty years to take these desires away from me. He [sic] didn't do it, and I can't give it up on my own. So what am I to do? Am I disqualified from the family of God because of my own peculiar curse? It seems to me that if I could overcome my sins through my own efforts then Jesus didn't need to shed his blood and die for me. I don't believe that I can add to what Jesus did for me by giving up crossdressing. That would amount to maintaining my salvation by works when the Bible teaches us that we are saved by grace alone.

My wife will have absolutely nothing to do with my crossdressing. She says that she married a man, not a woman. Initially she thought that I was gay. I'm not sure what she thinks now. The only reason I told her about my need to wear women's clothes was because I was trying to come closer to her and just wanted to be honest. I didn't want to lie to her anymore and was tired of hiding this aspect of myself from her.

I truly love my two children and miss them terribly. My teenage daughter is very angry and will hardly speak to me. My young son doesn't like what I'm doing and wants me to give it up, just like I would turn from any other sin. He and I still have a relationship, and I have tried to explain to him that this is something that has been part of me all my life; I'm powerless to do anything about it. He and I hugged each other and cried today. I let him know how much I loved him and wished that I could be with him. I feel terribly guilty for the way this is affecting my children, but I must be who I am and somehow trust God to work out their lives and mine as well.

How do I come to grips with my dilemma? I need help to get through this difficult time in my life and find out who I really am in Christ. Am I in or out of God's kingdom? I want to go back to church, but I don't know how I can under the circumstances.

Rita's story is, unfortunately, typical of many transgendered persons who are raised in the environment of an unyielding, patriarchal religious system of belief. The presence of inner condemnation, a lack of self-acceptance, the certainty of a "curse," and a misguided conviction that transgender desires are somehow "sinful" are often characteristic of such a destructive paradigm. Rita seems to be convinced that her differently gendered desires and behaviors are evil and ungodly in some way, and it's saddening to think of the negativity that she has internalized as a result of her belief system. She is psychologically immersed in a "religious based legalism that disregards human need"[6] and is obviously paying a heavy personal price for that spiritually and emotionally unhealthy immersion. Good people have been unnecessarily wounded by a religion that systematically and unjustly, yet very efficiently, teaches them to despise themselves for what they are. Situations like this tell us that sometimes we may have to let go of our socioreligious ideas of who we "should" be in order to discover and accept who we truly are.

A large part of Rita's ongoing struggle between her faith and her internal transgendered orientation reflects a traditional misapplication of a specific scripture passage. The prohibition against crossdressing in Deuteronomy 22:5 is contextually explained by many respected biblical scholars as a warning against various Canaanite orgiastic cult practices that were in vogue during the particular historical period and geographic location in which the injunction was written. According to this explanation the totally harmless behavior of crossdressing was not inherently abominable in and of itself; it was, however, to be avoided by the Israelites because of its idolatrous association with the worship of other regional gods. It had absolutely nothing to do with a legitimate gender variant orientation or expression—the concept of an internalized psychoemotional orientation was completely unknown in that historical period—but rather served as a religious hedge against the encroachment of alternative, forbidden social and religious practices.

Another explanation for the inclusion of this particular verse in the Hebrew canon is that Israel seemed to be preoccupied with distinctions between the genders. This was probably due to the patriarchal nature of that society. Males were determined to keep the upper hand in every aspect of community life, so men and women were forbidden from identifying with each other in ways that might potentially create any form of gender ambiguity or confusion leading to the diminishing of male dominance.

Of course, there are other interpretations and explanations for this particular Deuteronomic scriptural passage as well, and their existence serves only to demonstrate that no one knows precisely what the verse truly meant at that time, in that place, for the people to whom it was addressed, and what its relevance (if any) might be for us today. To take this verse out of its historical and geographical context, to interpret it literally, and then to conveniently and selectively use it as a weapon against those who exhibit a legitimate transgender orientation is, at best, spiritually arrogant and unfeeling. When carried to its extreme it becomes an example of idolatry, contradicting Jesus' message of love and inclusion. Extrapolation of contemporary meaning from scriptural passages is a time-honored tradition within Christianity, but such extrapolation should always be done in an attempt to lift people up, not tear them down.

THE EFFECTS OF TRANSGENDERPHOBIA

The existence of transgenderphobia is a stark reality in our society and in the church today. The result is oppression that continually and pervasively directs itself toward very specific targets. Transgenderphobic oppression requires four specific components in order to become internalized. Those elements are (1) prejudice, (2) misinformation, (3) isolation, and (4) bipolarized gender bias.[7]

These internalized transgenderphobic components in Rita's life are manifested in her lack of self-worth and her inability to love and accept herself as a unique, blessed, and gender-gifted human being created in the image of God. She has very effectively internalized the prejudice, misinformation, and rampant transgenderphobia that her society and her church have taught her so well, and she is suffering greatly because of it.

Gender variant people have been and continue to be rejected by society, but that is nothing compared to the level of rejection they have usually received from the "Christian" community. Is it any wonder that so many transgendered people have learned to hate the church, the Bible, and anything else considered "Christian"? After all, they are only behaving reciprocally according to the way they have been treated. Many transgendered Christians feel as though they have been disenfranchised, exiled, rejected, and ostracized—and, frankly, they have every right to feel that way. The church's record in such situations is hardly a shining example of God's inclusive love for all people. Gary David Comstock, a gay Christian seminary graduate, captured the feelings of many gender variant Christians when he wrote: "I find that the church remains the place, or certainly a prominent place, where I am least comfortable..., the place where I still feel defensive and least encouraged to share the most meaningful and intimate parts of my life. The church remains for me the place where the lump still tightens in my throat, where my stomach still knots in anticipation of rejection and difficulty."[8] The religious establishment has sown discord, persecution, and oppression for the differently gendered, so it should not surprise us that some transgendered persons flatly and bitterly reject the institution of Christianity for what they correctly perceive to be blatant hypocrisy and injustice directed toward them.

One of the first parables of Jesus I learned as a child was of the Prodigal Son. I used to believe that gender variant

people represented the prodigals, that we were simply expected to stop our "sinning," and that we were supposed
to come back to the "normality" of the church's loving
embrace whenever we were finally ready to renounce our
"depraved" transgendered behaviors in favor of a more
"socially acceptable lifestyle." Over time, I have come to
understand that it is the institutional church that is truly
the prodigal. Transgendered people have, for the most part,
never really desired to leave the church; instead, it's the
church that has shunned and abandoned *us!* Disenchanted
gender variant Christians might take heart from these words
of Jim May:

> Quite simply, the Christian life is about *Christ,* and not
> about religion, churches, groups, parachurch organi-
> zations, or even Christianity. There is a huge difference
> between the religion of Christianity and Christ.
>
> The religion of the Pharisees was based on the truth
> of the Old Testament, the word of God, as perceived by
> the Hebrews. The problem is that it became a religion
> at the expense of God. The same thing is happening
> today through accepted systems of evangelicalism and
> denominationalism that steal the life of Jesus while
> using His name. It just seems to be human nature
> to reduce religion to something we can control and
> understand without mystery.[9]

This overemphasis on rigid, soul-destroying, humanly defined religion at the expense of God-given, loving, accepting, Christ-centered spirituality and divine mystery has
been the bane of existence for many transgendered Christians over the centuries. Although negativity and oppression
have historically been directed at the gender variant community by Christianity, many differently gendered persons
(including me) still love and care deeply for the church.
We recognize that despite its aberrations and human im-
perfections it is still the Body of Christ and is thus an
important, even necessary, presence in our lives. We want

to remain within the church, though it often becomes extremely difficult to reconcile the love and acceptance of God for all persons with the actions and attitudes of the Christian community toward the gender variant. The situation is reminiscent of these lines from a medieval manuscript: "The church is a great deal like Noah's ark: if it weren't for the storm outside, you couldn't stand the stench inside." The time has come for the institutional church to recognize and admit its guilt in this unholy and unhealthy process of oppression, to honestly repent of its ungodly, heretical, idolatrous actions and attitudes toward transgendered persons, and to transform itself into the compassionate reflection of Christ that it was always intended to be.

OVERCOMING NEGATIVE RELIGIOUS IDEAS

Jesus was the absolute personification of compassion, especially for the poor, the oppressed, the outcasts, and other social outlaws. His compassionate actions, of course, made him very unpopular with the powerful religious and political leaders of his day. Jesus always went out of his way to demonstrate acceptance and inclusive love for those whom the establishment deemed unworthy. Compassion, however, "isn't the mushiness of do-gooders. Instead it is loving kindness, first for yourself and then for others. When you operate from this compassion you nurture your own ability, recognizing your own creativity and that of others."[10] If the Christian church is to embody Christlike qualities, it must learn the value and significance of compassion as Jesus expressed it.

Compassion, according to Marcus Borg,

> strikes some people as a "weak" value.... Thus it is important to underline that compassion does not mean simply being "nice." Nor does it mean "letting people off the hook," as if one would say in every situation,

"I understand," and never hold anybody accountable. The strength of compassion as a value can be seen by looking at its opposites: hatred, abuse, brutality, injustice; indifference, selfishness, self-righteousness, hardness of heart; racism, sexism, classism, militant nationalism, and so forth. To advocate compassion is to stand against these. Thus it is not a "weak" value that tolerates everything.[11]

In a sense, compassion is almost more notable for what it is *not* than for what it is.

Transgendered Christians need to recognize that because of who we are and what we do we have been made the victims of an insidious effort to instill fear, guilt, shame, and inferiority into our lives. The presence of guilt and shame acts as a cultural controlling mechanism, an effective device that tends to reduce or diminish the quality of the gender variant life experience for us. Guilt and shame, when associated with a differently gendered appearance or behavior, are socialized limitations that are placed upon the transgendered by a nonunderstanding culture. We must also recognize that "shame differs from guilt. As noted family therapist and theologian John Bowman has said, 'Guilt is, 'I made a mistake.' Shame is, 'I *am* a mistake.' "[12] Those who are differently gendered should know that—no matter what we may have been taught—it is *not* a mistake, a sin, or a moral failing to appear, feel, or behave in a gender variant manner. And most importantly, *we are not a mistake! We are precious, infinitely valuable human beings made in the image of our God, and no one has the right to attempt to convince us otherwise.*

Much of the moral and spiritual dilemma for conscientious transgendered Christians stems from arbitrary cultural and religious standards that have been formulated by fallible human beings, standards that are often imposed and enforced in a capricious and less-than-just manner. As Stephen Beers reminds us, however:

Why should you hold yourself to a moral standard that isn't adhered to by many of the very people who profess and uphold that same standard? Why should you try to adhere to a standard of moral perfection while the people who created the standard pick and choose their sins as it suits them?... In the end, the purity of your soul will not be determined by someone else's moral standard; it will be determined by you, your life, your conscience, and your God.[13]

The vignettes of Cynthia, Tracy, Philip, and Rita demonstrate the need for a transgendered liberation theology, one that can help to free the spirits of differently gendered persons while allowing them to become all they are capable of being in Christ. The experiences of these gender variant people within the church have been detrimental to their sense of worth and to their relationships with their faith communities. Unfortunately, such experiences are not at all uncommon. Theologian Dorothee Soelle has coined the term "Christofascism" to refer to the violence done by Christians to those whom they have judged to be "wrong."

In 1949 the play *South Pacific* debuted on Broadway and was an instant hit; many of its songs quickly became some of the most loved in all of American musical theater. However, one of the songs from that musical, "You've Got to Be Carefully Taught," was considered highly controversial for that time because it dealt with an interracial romance between an American soldier and a young Polynesian woman. Oscar Hammerstein's words ring as true today as they did in 1949, and they can surely be applied to the oppression that many transgendered persons suffer at the hands of so-called Christians within the institutional church. Bigotry is still bigotry, no matter what the form. The lyrics of this song tell us, "You've got to be taught to hate and fear... you've got to be carefully taught." For too long our churches have carefully instructed us to hate and fear anyone who differs from the "acceptable" religious status quo.

JADE DEVLIN'S STORY

I'd like to end this chapter with a different kind of personal story, one of hope and affirmation that indicates the possibilities for living a happy, fulfilled life as a transgendered Christian. Jade C. Devlin is a very bright, young male-to-female crossdressing Christian. She is also an MIT graduate with a wonderfully self-deprecating sense of humor and has done much good in Jesus' name for many within the transgender community. She shares her faith journey with us:

Countless people have asked me how I reconciled my faith with my crossdressing, how I overcame my feelings of religious guilt, and how I learned to accept myself in spite of my Christianity. These have always seemed bizarre questions to me. Reconciled? I have never believed that God opposed crossdressing. Accept myself? Without Christ, I don't know how I would ever have had the strength. Guilt? God has always been my way out of guilt, not into it. I feel like a skydiver being asked how she reconciled her skydiving with her parachute.

When I was in third grade, "release time" classes were available to students in my public school. Students could take an hour out of their school day to spend in classes at their church. I took a sign-up form, selected a church at random, and told my mom to sign it. She was a little bewildered; active belief was totally outside our world, much less active worship. None of my family or friends had ever spoken with me about God. I don't know how I even got the idea that there was a God to be fascinated with, but my fascination was real.

Anyway, my mom reselected a church, choosing one that my step-great-aunt attended—she was my closest family connection to an active churchgoer—and let me go. It was a tiny Episcopalian congregation dominated by gentle little old ladies, and I took to it with zeal. There was barely any youth or youth program, but I didn't mind; I was not exactly a social butterfly.

This enthusiasm crystallized into commitment and acceptance gradually over the next few years. I can only pinpoint one spiritual turning-point moment, somewhere around age eleven. I was serving as acolyte, and part of the Sermon on the Mount was being read. Somehow, the real authority of Jesus came through the text, plowing past the intervening centuries. The demands were so impossible, so absurd, and yet so very deeply right, and I knew that I was hearing the words of the Son of God. After that, it felt much less like worship was something I was doing—more like it was something God was doing to me.

Now for the dark side of the story. I was an extremely teasable kid. Small, clumsy, gentle to an extreme, studious, obedient. A classic nerd. I was reading newspapers at age three, wearing glasses at age five—a hopeless goody two-shoes, everything kids love to hate. Looking back, it's a wonder my peers weren't more hostile than they were. Anyway, I didn't mind their contempt too much—I preferred being alone anyway—but I didn't quite have the courage to do anything to make it worse.

Like, for instance, talk about my belief in God. Devotion to Christ would obviously be the last straw for a kid who was already disgustingly "good." I got teased for my faith, along with everything else, and I responded by becoming something of a closeted Christian. I couldn't really keep it a secret, but I could avoid bringing it up, and I did.

The funny thing is that, when I was being teased for believing, I really felt "bad" about it. I felt like believing was something I really should be ashamed of. I felt guilty. I felt wrong.

It took me too long to shake off that attitude. It wasn't until my sophomore year at MIT that I really confronted my fear of other people's contempt. God taught me how foolish it was to believe that truth and clear judgment could be absorbed from the prejudices and assumptions of the people around me. Since then, I think I've done pretty well at coming out of the closet as a Christian, with God's help.

And now, what about the crossdressing? For years I stifled all my thoughts about it, with one delightful and terrifying exception. I strangled my impulses and didn't even think about the fact that I was strangling them— never stopped to consider whether those thoughts were a part of my identity, much less a legitimate part. Fear was driving me, of course, fear of human contempt. I was so deep in contempt already, already known for countless "effeminate" characteristics, how could I even think of doing something so explicitly feminine?

I did not, for one moment, imagine that my fear was a fear of God. I knew very well the difference between fear of God and fear of man. I knew that fear of people made me ashamed to worship, and the same fear of the same people made me afraid to crossdress.

There are a lot of disadvantages to raising yourself Christian in a non-Christian environment, but there's one big advantage: you learn that our ways are not His ways. You learn that going with the flow is not going toward the Father. You learn that defying common wisdom and public opinion is not only permissible, but it's often the only way to obey God.

And so my coming out of the closet as a Christian paved the way for accepting myself as a crossdresser. The courage God taught me to live explicitly for Him was gradually spreading to other, less important parts of my life. It might have eventually gotten as far as my buried crossdressing yearnings. The process got a jump-start, though, after I met my wife. She is the most amazing, bold, unconventional person I have ever known, and absorbing just a drop of her courage changed me forever.

Thus, when I finally began seriously to crossdress, there was hardly any struggle to it. I had already fought that battle. I already knew that some fear is not worthy of being heeded.

I have long tried to offer every aspect of my life to God, to ask Him to use it to His purposes. Feeling a little silly, I offered my crossdressing to Him the same way. It seemed like an empty offering. God needed me in a dress? What, He needed some comic relief?

A few weeks later, using the Internet, I was amazed to learn that there were crossdressers who felt like Christ was a burden upon them. People who felt like God stood shoulder-to-shoulder with the playground bullies who kept me hiding myself for so long. Scanning one crossdresser's anguished posting, I felt God's voice very firmly. "You promised me."

Never make God a promise casually.

I wrote that crossdresser a letter with a few words of comfort and some second-grade Sunday school theology. Amazingly enough, it helped. So I did again, and again, with more and more people. I set up a website to broadcast what I found myself repeating. I set up an electronic mailing list so that other transgendered Christians could make uplifting connections to one another. I finally started sharing my faith energetically, and it was good.

And I am far from alone. Christians have become much more visible in the transgendered community. Two years ago, many people who wrote me were amazed to meet an-other transgendered Christian; they had believed they were the only ones in existence. I hardly ever hear that sentiment anymore. Instead, I hear of people involved in ministries and outreaches I never dreamed of.

I am writing this in 1999. I have been amazed and humbled by what I have seen God do so far. There is much more I am yearning and praying for. I still see trans-gendered Christians who find sorrow in Christ instead of joy. I still see transgendered non-Christians who believe that Christians are their enemies. I still see hearts closed to God because people believe that He comes bearing a dress code.

But, God willing, this shall pass.[14]

Even though I may not fully agree with some of her more traditional views of God (and I'll say more about such theological perspectives in the next chapter), I deeply respect Jade Devlin and appreciate her efforts on behalf of others. In the time that I have known her, she has unfailingly offered hope and support to those with whom she has come in contact; many transgendered persons have benefited from her willingness to reach out in Jesus' name. Jade is a wonderful example of how the church might well begin ministering to the differently gendered in love: it could begin by simply trying to meet a perceived need and then watch as ministry opportunities present themselves, for they invariably will.

7

A TRANSGENDERED CHRISTIAN CHURCH?

I FIND THE DIFFICULTIES experienced by many transgendered individuals within the context of the church,
though deeply saddening and often infuriating, to also
be somewhat ironic. This is because I am convinced that
the Christian church is struggling and, indeed, has always
struggled with an essentially unacknowledged but highly
significant transgendered identity of its own. While this
concept is admittedly somewhat controversial and almost
assuredly outside the usual frame of reference of most
church members, I offer this thesis for consideration and
base it upon observations that will become more apparent
as we proceed.

ANDROCENTRISM IN THE CHURCH

"Transgenderism," writes J. J. Allen, "like feminism, ar-
gues that gender, or what we often call masculinity and
femininity, has no logical or necessary connection to one's
biological sex. Therefore, men and women should be able
to cross over between masculinity and femininity as they
please."[1] Contrary to such an enlightened, liberating approach to gender expression it is no secret that the Christian
church has always functioned as a primarily patriarchal and
androcentric, or male-oriented, institution. It is generally
agreed that this has occurred in large part because, at least
from historical and biological perspectives, Jesus Christ was

indisputably a male. In addition, the society from which the Christian church sprang was highly patriarchal and the status of women was officially secondary. Thus the clergy, the church leadership, has always been primarily male, even exclusively so in some denominations, in my opinion to the detriment of all concerned. The Christian church desperately needs many more strong, competent female as well as openly gay, lesbian, bisexual, and transgendered clergypersons to complement the already existing male clergy. In this way our spiritual leaders may symbolically represent and physically embody a more complete, comprehensive, and balanced picture of the fullness of God.

In addition, the church has traditionally taught that the disciples of Jesus were male. Seldom is the importance of female disciples mentioned from the pulpits of our churches. Even though there were clearly disciples of Christ who were women, as delineated in various New Testament passages (e.g., Luke 8:1–3; Luke 10:38–42; Mark 3:14; Mark 15:40–41, etc.), mainstream religion has never really acknowledged them as such or accorded them the status that the male disciples have enjoyed. Even God is primarily presented in scripture as male, various feminine biblical references and analogies to our non-gender-specific Creator notwithstanding.[2] The doctrines, dogmas, and various traditions of the church have traditionally revolved around a core masculine identity, historically expressed and articulated through references to God the Father, Jesus the Son, and the usually masculine Holy Spirit.

It has become a source of fascination and great personal comfort to me that the person of the Holy Spirit was perceived and identified as feminine in the original Hebrew, though it has been rendered gender-neutral in later Greek translations of those scriptures. The Hebrew term for spirit, *ruach*, also means breath or wind, and is usually considered to be feminine in its gender. The institutional church, however, has done a most effective job in covering up, ignoring, or minimizing this information. Despite the fact that a slowly growing percentage of individual church congregations make attempts to use inclusive language when speaking of the Creator, God is still almost always referred to as "He," with only a few exceptions, in our mainstream Christian denominations. As a result, most church members tend to gravitate, almost by default, toward a more masculine image in their personal concept of the Creator.

THE CHURCH'S TRANSGENDERED PARADOX

Despite all this testosterone-laden religious rhetoric, I find it very interesting and occasionally even perversely amusing that the Christian church is quite clearly identified in scripture as a bride, usually as the "Bride of the Lamb" or the "Bride of Christ." The symbol of a bride is often used metaphorically in scripture to denote the nearest, firmest, most sure and loving relationship—a marriage—that exists between God and true believers (see, e.g., Ps. 45:6; Zech. 3:1; Matt. 9:15; Matt. 25:1; Rev. 21:9, 22:6). This most overtly feminine of images is seemingly totally at odds with the traditional androcentric identity of the institutional church, and it makes for a wonderful and even delightfully incongruous juxtaposition of gender-based identities. The paradox is quite remarkable in its implications for the Christian community and for each of us as individuals. The problem for the institutional church is that a tension clearly exists between these opposing polarities of socialized gender identification. On the one hand, the church has a traditionally vested interest in promoting and protecting a masculine identity (e.g., witness the difficulty that Roman Catholicism has confronted in insisting upon a male-only priesthood, or that highly patriarchal Protestant denominations such as the Southern Baptist Convention have with the idea of ordaining female pastors). On the other hand, there's no getting around the numerous scriptural references that indicate that the Christian church, the body of believers, is to assume the quintessentially feminine role of "bride" in its intimate relationship with God. This apparent psychological, emotional, and spiritual clash of gender roles and identities (with all their sexual overtones) appears to be remarkably similar to the internal struggles that many transgendered persons experience as they confront the reality of their differently gendered status. Evidently, the church is also going through its own dilemma with regard to gender; I somehow find that comforting and reassuring. If the powerful institution of the Christian church itself has difficulty in dealing with its own internal brand of transgenderism, then surely there's hope for those of us who are gender variant and love the church but struggle with the complexities that such a scenario creates.

It's quite possible and even probable that one of the reasons for the church's negative attitude toward transgendered people is due to the confusion and consternation that such persons represent for organized religion in general. The institutional church sometimes reminds me of a duck swimming on a pond: the duck may appear to be serene and controlled on the surface, but just beneath the water it is paddling frantically trying to maintain a semblance of equilibrium, decorum, and unified purpose.

It has always been a source of bittersweet amusement to me that we hear so much talk about unity in our churches but actually see so little of it. The idea of unity is wonderful in theory, but in practice it seems to be an extremely rare occurrence. Bringing people together to agree on *anything* of a religious nature seems to be a Herculean task. Sadly, many church leaders tend to emphasize and promote the idea of unity over love and integrity, perhaps hoping that some sort of common spiritual "truth" will mysteriously arise if a perceived consensus can only prevail on a particular issue. The concept of "unity" within religious circles often has more to do with serving and maintaining the status quo than with a common search for truth and justice. The church would do well to keep in mind that, as Bishop

Spong says, "unity is a very secondary virtue. Faithfulness and integrity [are] primary."[3]

FEARS, THREATS, AND REFLECTIONS

The Christian church seems to intuitively (albeit subconsciously, for the most part) recognize the existence of its innate gender-based paradox, and it very neatly manages to transfer or project its fears and reluctant concerns about its own transgenderism directly onto persons who are "different." The very presence of gender variant people within the church is a constant yet painful reminder to the institution of its internal struggles with gender identity. The reasons for negative religious attitudes toward the transgendered become quite clear when viewed from this perspective. This certainly doesn't make such discriminatory attitudes just or fair by any means and it surely doesn't absolve the church from blame, but it does help to explain the negative attitudes and oppressive behaviors.

The confusion over gender identity and the difficulties that result from it are an important, though largely unnoticed, part of the ongoing struggle for acceptance and respect that many differently gendered persons confront within the Christian church. As long as the church cannot (or refuses to) come to terms with its own uniquely transgendered status, it will surely be very difficult for the institution to fully accept and welcome those individuals who are gender variant. To be effective, the church must exist as a community of faith rooted in the concept of wholeness and right relationship among its members, and that cannot happen until the institution begins to accept and embrace its own diverse and differently gendered status as a naturally occurring part of life.

Our culturally derived notions of gender (and thus of society's male-dominated "order" which, according to the theological insistence of some, is "God-ordained") are always challenged whenever a person moves outside the accepted norms and takes on a differently gendered role. Difficulties are almost sure to arise whenever entrenched cultural mores or protected traditions are "threatened," and the church usually reacts to these perceived socio-religious threats with ignorance, fear, animosity, hostility, and defensiveness.

Society and, by extension, the Christian community, is moving inexorably toward a period of reaction to issues of gender/sexual minority inclusion. The questions are what kind and how much of a reaction it will be. Historically, the forces of positive change within the church have been furiously challenged by the forces of resistance to any change that might threaten the status quo. No one should expect the church's entrenched, male-dominated hierarchy to stand idly by and willingly allow transgendered persons to be welcomed and fully accepted into the Body of Christ without a struggle: "Something deeply destructive," says Bishop Spong, "is unleashed in some threatened human beings when they cannot keep the world from changing and in the process diminishing their power. They inevitably seek to destroy what they cannot control."[4]

The church is often simply reflecting the wider socio-cultural values related to gender that are so prevalent all around us. Any socially aware person knows that women are, unfortunately and unfairly, considered to be second-class citizens in this culture and thus within the Christian church. It should come as no great surprise to us that differently gendered persons are also ascribed second-class status by our primary social institutions. However, the combination of prevailing social gender norms and the institutional church's own internalized transgendered identity creates a quandary for the church—and certainly for the gender variant individual who desires to live within the framework of the Christian community.

Until the church, the Bride of Christ, can come to accept itself as a transgendered entity absolutely brimming with potential for God-breathed diversity and goodness, there will be ongoing difficulties concerning the widespread acceptance of differently gendered individuals within our institution.

A TRANSGENDERED CHRIST?

As an extension of our "transgendered church" thesis, let us briefly examine some of the characteristics that society has arbitrarily (and, to a degree, unjustly) deemed appropriate and acceptable for males and females. We can then compare those characteristics to some of the known behaviors that Jesus modeled for us during his life on earth. As we do so we will discover, interestingly enough, that Jesus manifested many behaviors and characteristics that could easily be considered "transgendered."

Here are a few characteristics that are generally considered "masculine" by our culture, although many males do not fit the stereotype that these qualities might suggest. In fact, very few, if any, males embody all of these characteristics at a given time:

- aggressive
- dominant
- decisive and systematic
- blunt and forceful
- commanding and direct
- dependable and courageous
- reliable
- strong and protective
- leader
- active and demanding
- determined and stubborn
- detached and impersonal
- practical and logical

- rough

Below is a short, and obviously incomplete, list of characteristics that our society typically labels "feminine." Again, we must hasten to add that most females do not (and probably wouldn't want to) fit the generalized social stereotype that these attributes suggest:

- passive
- receptive
- variable and capricious
- indirect and yielding
- obedient and accepting
- dependent, timid, and trusting
- weaker, seeking protection
- follower
- patient and enduring
- accommodating and changeable
- compassionate and involved
- emotional and intuitive
- gentle[5]

Now let us examine these characteristics and behaviors as they were exhibited in the life of Christ. Here are the ostensibly masculine qualities, with a brief assessment of their manifestations by Jesus:

- aggressive—yes, when appropriate
- dominant—no, at least not in the pejorative sense
- decisive and systematic— yes
- blunt and forceful—yes, when appropriate
- commanding and direct— yes
- dependable and courageous—yes, undoubtedly so
- reliable— yes

- strong and protective— yes
- leader—yes
- active and demanding—yes, when appropriate
- determined and stubborn—determined, yes; stubborn, no
- detached and impersonal— no
- practical and logical—yes
- rough— no

Finally, here are the feminine characteristics with a brief description of their manifestation in the life of Jesus:

- passive—yes, sometimes
- receptive— yes
- variable and capricious— no
- indirect and yielding—yes, sometimes
- obedient and accepting—yes
- dependent, timid and trusting—dependent, yes (but only upon God); timid, no; trusting, yes
- weaker and seeking protection—weaker, no; seeking protection, yes (but only by God, the source of strength)
- follower—yes (of Judaism and of God's will for his life)
- patient and enduring—yes
- accommodating and changeable—accommodating, yes; changeable, no
- compassionate and involved—yes, amazingly so
- emotional and intuitive—yes
- gentle—yes, exceptionally so

If these attributes are accepted as reasonably accurate social markers for the masculine and feminine genders, then becoming Christlike involves assuming some parts of both as well as rejecting parts of both gender paradigms. For example, Christian men who refuse to be gentle and emotional or Christian women who refuse to be courageous and decisive are effectively eliminating certain of Jesus' attributes from their lives. By the same token, Christian women who refuse to be rough or detached and impersonal are imitating Christ's behavior, and males who refuse to be weak or capricious are also emulating the characteristics of Jesus. If "transgendered" means crossing the lines of conventionally restrictive, socially enforced behavior and attitudes, we might make the case that God prefers all people to be "transgendered," at least in a broad sense, in order to embody these Christlike qualities in their lives.[6]

"Christology" refers to theological interpretation of the person and work of Christ. Transgendered Christians, the gender variant followers of Jesus, need to begin the development of a new and relevant approach to Christology, one that includes images of Christ that are meaningful to us. Theologian Eleanor McLaughlin, the vicar of Christ Church in South Barre, Massachusetts, takes the concept of a transgendered Christ to a startlingly new place:

> Jesus, who was and is both "historical fact" and symbol, a man, is like a "cross-dresser," one who is not "caught" by the categories.... Christians believe in a Jesus "dressed" in the flesh, that most female of symbols, and they believe in a God in man-flesh who behaves like a woman. This "transvestite" Jesus makes a human space where no one is out of place because the notion of place and gender has been transformed.[7]

McLaughlin's bold, transformative, and liberating new image of Christ as transvestite may make us a bit uncomfortable. But we need to be shaken out of our old, outmoded ideas about what Jesus is and, more importantly, what Jesus can be so that we can continually reimagine new possibilities for our lives in relationship with our God, a God of infinite possibilities. According to Marcus Borg:

The point is not that Jesus was a good guy who accepted everybody, and thus we should do the same (although that *would* be good). Rather, his teachings and behavior reflect an alternative social vision. Jesus was not talking about how to be good and how to behave within the framework of a domination system. He was a critic of the domination system itself. Indeed, that's the best explanation for why he was killed. He wasn't simply a nice inclusive fellow but a religious social prophet whose teaching, behavior, and social vision radically challenged the elites and the domination system of his day.[8]

The social and spiritual qualities that Jesus exhibited in his attitudes and behavior were directed toward transforming the established order. Jesus introduced a radically new way for people to treat each other. Gender and its various human manifestations are important aspects of that overall relational approach, both for Jesus in his day and for us as contemporary followers of Christ.

8

CHRISTIAN LIBERATION AND TRANSGENDERED PEOPLE

THE TRANSGENDERED IN OUR SOCIETY need to be freed from a destructive ideological paradigm of gender, one that has proven to be extremely successful at invalidating and trivializing the lives and experiences of gender variant people. This injurious paradigm has assumed mass proportions and is so culturally pervasive that most people never stop to think about the tremendous psychological, social, and spiritual harm that is being done daily to differently gendered persons through its sheer magnitude and ubiquitous presence. Author Larry Gross writes that the mass media in our society sustains a dominant ideology that minimizes "any presumed threat to the 'natural...' order of things." Consequently, gender minorities, much like other minorities in this society, are either "symbolically annihilated" by their invisibility or "kept in their places" by often inaccurate portrayals in the mass media. "Minority positions and interests which present radical challenges to the established order," says Gross, "will not only be ignored, they will be discredited."[1] Transgendered persons represent a radical challenge to the status quo of society, and certainly of the Christian church. Therefore, the gender variant are likely to be dismissed by our institutional authorities as irrelevant and inconsequential or perceived as threats to the fabric of the social order.

It is not my intention to foster a "victim mentality"

among transgendered Christians, nor do I wish my differently gendered sisters and brothers to think of ourselves as helpless or perpetual victims of the socioreligious establishment. We who are transgendered can—and must—find new ways to move from victimization into social and spiritual empowerment and self-fulfillment. While it is true that gender variant persons have often been the undeserving targets of discrimination and injustice in various forms, it is equally true that we are fully capable of being strong, healthy people who can contribute greatly to the betterment of society, the church, and our various communities.

THE GOOD NEWS OF LIBERATION

Liberation is an essential—perhaps *the* essential—element of the Gospel of Jesus Christ for human beings, and certainly for differently gendered human beings. Transgendered persons have been given an incredible gender-gift but, as is usually the case, along with a great gift comes great responsibility. Part of our responsibility includes recognizing and affirming the reality of the gender-gift itself, instead of denying or rejecting it. Seeking personal spiritual liberation through the good news of Jesus Christ will help us to accept our responsibilities and benefits as gender variant individuals, allowing us to more fully celebrate our transgendered orientation and identity as the true blessings from God that they are.

It is our well-being as gender variant persons created in the *imago Dei* that we are discussing, and that well-being is perhaps best expressed by the word *shalom*. *Shalom*, according to Marcus Borg, is

> a rich Hebrew word often translated as "peace" but meaning much more than the absence of war. It means well-being in a comprehensive sense. It includes freedom from negatives such as oppression, anxiety, and fear, as well as the presence of positives such as health,

prosperity, and security. *Shalom* thus includes a social vision: the dream of a world in which such well-being belongs to everybody.[2]

According to Webster, the word "liberate" means to set free, to release, or to change the status or ownership of something or someone. A Christian transgender theology of liberation should concern itself, at the very least, with issues such as:

- freeing differently gendered persons from institutionalized social and religious oppression;

- releasing gender variant people from the bondage of unwarranted sociocultural, intrapersonal, and spiritual negativity;

- transforming the current culturally imposed second-class status of the transgendered to one of acceptance and respect within the mainstream of society and its institutions, including (and even especially) the Christian church;

- recognizing and affirming the importance of the spiritual, psychoemotional, and social well-being of differently gendered individuals;

- pursuing justice, peace, happiness, and integrity for gender variant persons as intrinsically valuable human beings created in God's image.

Liberation always begins when someone makes a decision to refuse the imposed definitions of others. It then shifts toward active rebellion against those imposed definitions, moving toward the acquisition of personal power—power that offers new possibilities for achieving greater wholeness and individual and community fulfillment as human beings.

Once we have begun to refute the "outside" definitions that have been imposed on us by others we must take positive action on our own behalf against the oppressive status quo. It is not enough for us to pray, although prayer for strength and guidance is certainly important. We must take action and *do* something about our situation if we are to truly become free. God will help us and journey with us because God loves us; God is always on the side of the oppressed, but God also expects us to do our part in co-creating our own liberation. God is our cornerstone and our focus, not merely our assistant, in this effort. Our strength ultimately flows from the wellspring of our Creator, not from ourselves. That realization is what will give us power—internalized God-given power—to grow, to learn, to become, to do justice, to be assets to Christianity and the world, and to be more fully whole as we strive to live lives of integrity that will be pleasing to the One who so lovingly created us.

ADDRESSING OUR PAIN

Emotional, psychological, physical, economic, social, and spiritual pain has been a constant companion for differently gendered persons throughout the centuries. That pain is yet another reason why we need to develop a transgender liberation theology of our own. However, developing and implementing—"doing"—this theology will not be an easy task, either for us or for the institution of Christianity. This is because liberation theological movements, in Brock's words, "challenge the traditional self-understanding of the church."[3] Calls for paradigm shifts of this magnitude have been historically answered in the negative by institutions that perceive such changes as threats to their stability and status. As Gary David Comstock says, "We have to face squarely that our very lives, when lived openly and fully, fundamentally threaten the social order. When we begin to make decisions for ourselves instead of letting others tell us how we should live, we challenge those who have power at the expense of the disempowered and disenfranchised."[4]

Asian feminist theologian Kwok Pui Lan, professor of Christian theology and spirituality at Episcopal Divinity

School, was not specifically addressing transgendered Christian concerns when she wrote her essay "God Weeps with Our Pain," but her words are relevant here. Without attempting to co-opt the distinct oppressive situations that are unique to Asian women, I believe that Kwok also speaks to and for the differently gendered in many ways. Kwok states, "Women suffer from the millennia-old prejudices and discriminations of the male-dominated Eastern cultures, from rampant sociopolitical exploitations, and from their structural vulnerability. The big burdens join hand-in-hand to rob a woman of her personhood, to render her a nobody."[5] Kwok recognizes the need for people like herself to cry out for justice in the midst of their oppression, and her words ring true for gender variant people as well: "I only know that feminist theology in Asia will be a cry, a plea and an invocation. It emerges from the wounds that hurt, the scars that do not disappear, the stories that have no ending. Feminist theology in Asia is not written with a pen, it is inscribed on the hearts of many who feel the pain, and yet dare to hope."[6]

OUR PERSONAL RELATIONSHIP WITH GOD

Carter Heyward says that "Christians are called more than anything to be faithful, not 'right.' Faithful not to religions or creeds; faithful not to particular...institutions; and faithful certainly not to any tradition or custom that requires us to cast out or punish those who seem to us heretical, or wrong, in their beliefs or in their nonviolent customs and behavior."[7] We should not overly concern ourselves with being theologically or socially "correct," although it is always incumbent upon us as Christians to take thoughtful, responsible positions on social and spiritual issues. Instead, we need to focus our efforts and energies on being faithful to the law of love, on doing justice, and on creating right relationships.

CHRISTIAN LIBERATION AND TRANSGENDERED PEOPLE   103

We have unlimited access to God at all times and in all situations. Being liberated in our faith involves a recognition of God's accessibility for us, perhaps even outside of standard religious or institutional channels. Marcus J. Borg says,

> Jesus disclosed that the sacred is accessible apart from institutional mediation. In Jesus' social world, the official institutional mediator of the sacred was the temple in Jerusalem. Not only was the temple the place of God's presence but certain kinds of sins and impurities could be taken care of only through temple sacrifice. But Jesus (like his mentor John the Baptizer) affirmed the accessibility of God without temple mediation. He operated outside of institutional structures.[8]

Jesus is our prime example of a uniquely personal relationship with God. Such a relationship may, if required by circumstances, move outside the inflexible, established structures of religious institutions into the realm of individual spiritual communion with the God in whose image we were created. We don't always have to depend upon the whims of organized religion to know and experience God, although such knowledge and experience can occur within those institutions as well. Instead, we can be individually liberated into a place of holy personal relationship with our Creator, unfettered by the institutionalized religious constraints. Christian mystics have known the liberating experience of a personalized relationship with the divine for centuries, and that type of experience is still available for us today if we but seek it.

Our marginalized status within Christianity may be an impetus for some transgendered Christians to seek out exactly this kind of individualized relationship with God. That relationship may, in turn, lead us to a greater understanding of the importance of spiritual liberation. In his seminal book, *A Theology of Liberation*, Gustavo Gutiérrez reminds us that, "an awareness of the need for self-liberation

is essential to a correct understanding of the liberation process. It is not a matter of 'struggling for others,' which
suggests paternalistic and reformist objectives, but rather of
becoming aware of oneself as not completely fulfilled and
as living in an alienated society."

Gutiérrez, recognized by many as the father of liberation
theology, understands the spiritual life as a journey in which
we walk according to the Spirit (Romans 8):

> We make this spiritual journey, not as disembodied
> spirits but as flesh-and-blood creatures, located in a
> particular historic era and a specific social milieu. Liv-
> ing as a genuine disciple in the power of the Spirit
> requires a process of conversion. We must overcome
> our false consciousness and apathy by recognizing the
> pervasive power of social sin. Only then can we under-
> take effective action to create a society more responsive
> to human needs.[9]

Our culture is hostile to transgendered persons, and Christians must recognize the institutional church's historical
complicity in creating that climate of hostility. The only
effective way to begin the struggle against this cultural antagonism and animosity is to better understand our own
singular need for liberation. That understanding—a critical
part of our personal "conversion process"—will allow us
to take responsible, responsive action toward the creation
of a healthy social order and a Christian church that can
genuinely welcome and celebrate the diverse gender-gifts of
its members.

It is not my intention to minimize the importance of the
religious community or of the church as a viable mechanism
for our Christian spiritual expression. Indeed, rampant and
indiscriminate individualism has sometimes fostered a dangerous, even seductive, anti-institutional bias, encouraging
persons to think of themselves as autonomous entities that
can best find fulfillment through complete emancipation
from the Christian church. We must develop a construc-

tive, workable balance between human community and individual spiritual expression. We must affirm our sacred, highly personalized relationship with our Creator, as well as our community of faith. Both relationships—individual and communal—are necessary for us to maintain a sense of wholeness in our spiritual life as transgendered Christians.

THE LIBERATIVE STORY

I've heard it said that the reason God created human beings was because God loves stories. And what are our lives but a continuing series of stories? In constructing our theology of liberation for transgendered people, we should perhaps first examine the foundational story of liberation in the Judeo-Christian tradition. This is, of course, the biblical narrative of the release of the Israelites from Egyptian bondage and their passage to safety through the Red Sea as they journeyed toward the Promised Land (Exod. 1:1–15:21). It is also a tale of the conflict between the Egyptian Pharaoh's system of domination and Moses' (that is, God's) alternative social vision for God's people, a holy vision rooted in compassion, redemption, and salvation. Most Christians and practically all Jews are at least somewhat familiar with this story; it has been told and retold throughout the centuries in countless ways. Many of us remember Charlton Heston and Yul Brynner as Moses and Rameses, the two adversaries in the film *The Ten Commandments*, and more recently we have been offered Hollywood's take on the story in animated form, a film entitled *The Prince of Egypt*. This story has had an immense impact upon the world, especially in Judaism and Christianity. The ancient narrative of God's intervention on behalf of the Israelites at the Red Sea can also speak directly to the hearts and spirits of contemporary transgendered Christians.

The Hebrew scriptures tell us that the Israelite people were held captive as slaves in the land of Egypt under a cruel ruler called the pharaoh. God raised up a great prophet, Moses, who confronted this pharaoh and, through a miraculous series of events, brought about the release of the Israelites from their Egyptian captivity. However, the pharaoh quickly came to regret his decision to allow the Israelites to go free; he set out with his armies to recapture the Israelites and bring them back to Egypt as slaves once more. The people of Israel found themselves trapped at the shore of the Red Sea with the Egyptian armies bearing down upon them from behind. There appeared to be no escape route, and the Israelites were in obvious danger of being killed or returned to slavery.

At this point the story of divine intervention, leading to liberation for the nation of Israel, reaches its astonishing climax. God heard the despairing cries of the people and parted the waters of the Red Sea, allowing Moses and the Israelites to walk safely through the midst of the waters on dry land to the other shore. The sea remained parted until all the Israelites had crossed over. God miraculously made a way for them when there seemingly was no way. (To this day, "crossing over" to salvation remains a common theme of hope and inspiration for oppressed faith communities.) Then, as the Egyptians tried to follow, God caused the sea to come together again and Pharaoh's armies were drowned. In this archetypal story of liberation we see God moved to compassion and acting on behalf of an oppressed people, miraculously bringing them out of bondage and allowing them to cross over to salvific liberation from their oppressors.

(There are always those who ask about the other side of the story: What about the rank-and-file Egyptian soldiers? Did they all deserve to be drowned? Was it fair for God to simply wipe them out in one fell swoop in the waters of the Red Sea? What kind of a just and supposedly loving God would create an indiscriminate mass murder of such proportions? Things are not always as clear cut as they might first appear or as we were taught in Sunday school. All sorts of questions might be raised regarding the seemingly offhanded and brutal way that God dealt with the Egyptians, not to mention the apparently God-ordained wholesale slaughter of Israel's neighboring tribes later on as documented in the continuing saga of the Hebrews—but those are subjects for another time.[10])

CONSIDERING OUR THEOLOGY

To better understand the momentous concept of liberation as it applies to the life of socially or spiritually oppressed Christians, we must briefly examine the concept of "liberation theology" itself. The term "theology" simply means "the study of God," while "liberation" obviously refers to being set free or, as in the case of the Israelites, to being released from some type of bondage. Liberation theology concerns itself with the study of God as a proactive agent in the lives of persons who struggle to be set free from oppression. Liberation theology's primary tenet is that God, rather than being neutral, is always on the side of the oppressed. In "liberation theology" God is viewed as the liberator of the oppressed. Oppression in any form is seen as "sin." Resistance to oppression—the struggle against sin—thus becomes God's will for our lives.

As we see in the Exodus story, the triumph of divine justice over oppression becomes God's liberating victory over sin itself. Whenever someone is freed from oppression or subjugation, God is glorified because sin has been overcome. The liberated person can then look back on that event as a pivotal moment of divine intervention, an experience that will be remembered and venerated for its redemptive, life-giving implications. The Feast of Passover, celebrating God's miraculous deliverance of the Hebrews from Egyptian bondage, is just such a beloved mechanism of remembrance for the Jewish community to this day.

This is the kind of liberating paradigm that we transgendered people need to adopt and claim as our own. For too long we have been the victims of systemic social and spiritual injustice; it is now time for us to look not to the misguided socioreligious institutions that would enslave and oppress us but directly to the loving, life-giving God who created us for freedom, for salvation, and for right relationship. For us, says Stephen Breck Reid, "the issue is whether the community will internalize the will and perspective of 'Pharaoh' or whether we will internalize the will and perspective of the God of freedom, who has set us free."[11]

TRADITION

Although I may have given the opposite impression, I do not summarily dismiss tradition as useless or irrelevant. However, there are indeed some elements of religious tradition that I find to be antithetical to a healthy, unfettered exploration of one's spirituality.[12]

The combination of Spirit and unquestioning adherence to religious tradition for tradition's sake has sometimes proven to be highly volatile. People sometimes say that something must be done a certain way because "that's the way we've always done it." We also hear a great deal about the need for strict adherence to "traditional values." The term is a euphemism, code language for a religio-political theocratic agenda of exclusivity. Borg writes:

> The contrast between tradition and Spirit does not mean that tradition has no value or that it is always an obstacle. Rather, the indictment is against one way that tradition can function. Namely, when tradition is thought to state the way things really are, it becomes the director and judge of our lives; we are, in effect, imprisoned by it. On the other hand, tradition can be understood as a pointer to that which is beyond tradition: the sacred. Then it functions not as a prison but as a lens.[13]

Tradition can become a prison, or even an idol, if we allow it. However, using Borg's enlightened perspective we can begin to view the Exodus story not as part of imprisoning or idolatrous tradition but as a spiritual lens through which we can more readily look "beyond" and perceive how God moves and works in people's lives. Gender variant people need to begin creating our own traditions, ones firmly established in the healthy understanding, full acceptance, and celebration of our uniquely transgendered lives and our rich, sacred, gender variant experiences. We need to develop new traditions that point us to the holy and the life-affirming rather than forcing us back toward circumstances and situations that are oppressive and unjust. As we do so, the profoundly human stories of our community will provide fertile ground for our growing theological understanding.

THE IMPORTANCE OF SCRIPTURE

Any legitimate Christian theology includes the consideration of scripture as a necessary component. It might be helpful in this context, especially for differently gendered persons, to heed the words of Filipino liberation theologian Eleazar Fernandez, associate professor of constructive theology at United Theological Seminary of the Twin Cities:

> Theological construction, if it wants to be called Christian theology, must consider the Bible or Scripture as indispensable; it is a classic text for Christian theology. However, its usefulness for a liberating theological construction is also dependent on how it is construed as a source. I suggest that the Bible or Scripture, as an important source for theological construction and in particular for the theology of struggle, should be viewed relative to life and more specifically to the life of the community. Life takes first place![14]

Life takes first place! If that inspiring and liberating idea ever becomes prevalent in our churches, the self-appointed gatekeepers of pious exclusivity and enforced religious conformity have reason to fear.

Renita J. Weems, professor of theology at Vanderbilt University Divinity School, writes:

> The Bible's status within the Christian community as an authoritative text whose content is seen as binding upon one's existence always has been a complicated matter. Its role for marginalized readers—especially those who read the Bible in order to get some idea of who they are in the presence of God or who they are in relation to other people—is even more complicated and problematic.[15]

The problems arise because marginalized readers inevitably come into conflict with the prevailing modes of operation and the oppressive methodologies enforced by those in positions of power within our religious institutions. When this happens, it becomes essential for us to remember that the Bible is *our* book, too; it doesn't belong only to the religious leaders or the molders of popular opinion. The scriptures are a gift to us from a loving God, much like life itself, and are to be used as tools to assist us in moving ever closer to the One who created us as unique and beloved differently gendered persons. Fernandez further writes:

> Life is not for the Bible, but the Bible is for life; it should promote life, be at the service of life, not the other way around. Faithfulness to the Bible does not mean fitting one's life to biblical times; nor is it measured by claims to originality or by a meticulous process of repetition, but by the pursuit of a life-generating meaning that is reproduced as our context engages in a dialectical interplay with the text. The Bible as a whole "contains something of truth not because of its origins, but because it liberates people now from specific forms of oppression."[16]

We transgendered people obviously need to focus our efforts on the development of a theology that views the Bible as a valuable tool for life and liberation, not as the "inerrant, infallible, indisputable, inarguable Word of God," a weapon to bludgeon us into gender-based submission to arbitrary socioreligious expectations. The Bible, writes liberation theologian Carlos Mesters, "can be a force for liberation or a force for oppression. If it is treated like a finished monument that cannot be touched, that must be taken literally as it is, then it will be an oppressive force."[17] If Christianity and the Bible do not affirm life and liberation, then they are essentially useless and irrelevant to us. A restrictive, literalist, fundamentalist interpretive approach to scripture can serve only as a weapon of oppression and not as a tool of liberation.

SCRIPTURE, EXPERIENCE, TRADITION, AND REASON

A specifically transgendered biblical hermeneutic will incorporate the transgender experience into its approach. But if we are to adopt such an interpretive perspective we must first recognize and affirm the value and legitimacy of our lives as differently gendered persons. Mesters writes:

> In the past we members of the clergy expropriated the Bible and got a monopoly on its interpretation. We took the Bible out of the hands of the common people, locked it with a key, and then threw the key away. But the people have found the key and are beginning again to interpret the Bible. And they are using the only tool they have at hand: their own lives, experiences, and struggles.[18]

Mesters has recognized the significance of this grassroots, experiential, and highly contextual interpretive approach to scripture; differently gendered people need to use a similar approach to develop our own interpretations of the

Bible. Our transgendered lives, experiences, and struggles can offer valuable insights into scriptural interpretation for others and for ourselves.

Latina and *Mujerista* theologian Ada María Isasi-Díaz, associate professor of theology and ethics at Drew University, reminds us:

> If one does not risk articulating some of the understandings that are part of the lived-experience of the community of faith, of the theologizing community to which one belongs, that faith and theology will never become explicit, will never become a part of the normative theological understandings of the Christian community at large and will remain marginal even for the community out of which they come.[19]

In short, our experiences as gender variant human beings are valid, and they must necessarily shape our faith and theology as the beloved transgendered people of God. There is no discernibly strong presence (or even a weak presence, for that matter!) of differently gendered persons in the theological marketplace at this time, and so it becomes even more vital that we work toward the development of a legitimately transgendered liberative theology that will inform our lives as persons who seek and desire a complete relationship with our Creator and with Christ's church.

Isasi-Díaz was referring specifically to Latinas when she wrote the following but, like those of Kwok Pui Lan, her words apply directly to the differently gendered:

> Those in the Bible who struggled for liberation, for survival, including Jesus, are one of the few "reality checks" that Latinas have. Society questions our reality, how we understand it and deal with it. Society alienates Latinas and marginalizes us because our cultural values and understandings are different. We are not willing to participate in society on the terms of the dominant culture because those terms are oppressive

for us as well as for other marginalized groups. Anyone, including biblical persons, who has gone through situations similar to ours serves as an encouragement to us to believe in ourselves and our communities. All such persons and examples help us know that we are not imagining things; that though we are often rendered invisible by those who have power, we do not cease to exist.[20]

DOING OUR THEOLOGY

We need to find meaning and value for our lives as differently gendered people of God despite the insistent social questioning and religious denial of our gender variant reality. A transgendered liberation theology can be a way for us to discover and articulate such meaning and value. Constructing this theology will require hearts and minds that are open to the Holy Spirit's leading, hearts and minds that will actively and honestly:

- seek justice;

- recognize the dangers and name the injustices that exist for transgendered persons in the church, while at the same time continuing to affirm the Christian community as a potentially good and viable vehicle for God's work on earth;

- work toward genuine mutuality and reciprocity in relationship, not some perceived "unity" at the expense of truth or justice for all people;

- seek the strength and insight that come from the reading and application of scripture within a liberative context; and

- seek to know the joy of a fulfilling personal relationship with God in Jesus Christ, a relationship based completely and unconditionally in love.

Carter Heyward writes movingly of the life that we have been given, first as human beings and then as Christians:

> Even amid its fragments and particularities, it is a common life with roots in God. Of that I am sure. And several other things I know: that we humans are basically good and so too is the world; that we and the world, like our Sacred Source, are badly broken by evil; and that we need one another to heal. Socially and politically, spiritually and morally, this is our life's work—to be healers and liberators of and with one another.[21]

We are intimately, inextricably connected in a mysterious, sacred bond with each other and with the One who created us. When we strive to heal the brokenness in ourselves and in our relationships, then we do God's work in this world.

9

ELEMENTS OF EMANCIPATION FOR TRANSGENDERED CHRISTIANS

SOME OF US have very successfully internalized the prevailing notion: "You can be Christian. You can be transgendered. But you can't be both Christian *and* transgendered." This unholy and damaging premise is wrong. It is entirely possible to be both Christian and transgendered. I know, because I live out that reality every day, and so do many, many others (more than you know, I assure you). We don't have to jump through any hoops, sit before a review panel or a church board, be subject to a committee vote or denominational decree, or pass a theological litmus test to be gender variant Christians. Despite the ignorance and the transgenderphobic attitudes, we can rest secure in the knowledge that our Creator actively desires and purposely seeks a loving relationship with each one of us. Our God will never stop reaching out to us no matter who we are, how we identify and present ourselves in terms of gender, or what we wear. As Jade Devlin put it, God doesn't come bearing a dress code.

The realization that God loves and accepts us just as we are can ultimately be the catalyst and impetus for our own acceptance and sense of self-worth as transgendered Christian individuals. Once we have genuinely accepted this truth it becomes easier to begin working toward wholeness, spiritual growth, and the liberation of our hearts, souls, and minds that we seek through Jesus Christ. The knowledge of this unconditional acceptance by our Creator is incredibly empowering, and we need to recognize and affirm the strength that becomes available to us as the result of this awareness. As we grow more cognizant of this sacred, God-given strength, we can also become more confident in our own spiritual gifts and abilities to act as the hands of Jesus Christ in our world.

BECOMING AWARE OF PREJUDICE

A relatively small percentage of persons have highly negative, vindictive, and overtly hostile views toward the differently gendered, and we must be aware that these people mistakenly consider the existence of gender variant persons to be some sort of imminent danger to them and to society at large. Such prejudice apparently serves an important, though misguided, psychological function for the personalities of these individuals: it gives them a kind of psychoemotional comfort when their ideas about traditional gender roles are challenged in any way. Those "gender challenges" greatly upset some persons, quite possibly because they strike a little too close to home. After all, as Rik Isensee reminds us, "People tend not to recognize things they dislike about themselves. Instead, they project those negative qualities onto others."[1]

Prejudice against the transgendered may represent a disowned or subconscious side of some individuals, a side that invokes fears or insecurities regarding their understanding of what it means to be a man or a woman. They feel threatened by our perceived transgressions of the culture's fixed gender expectations. Rather than recognizing their own internal ambivalence in these matters, they perceive the threat as coming from the outside and, more specifically, from transgendered persons.[2] Such challenges have the capacity to create intense feelings of hostility in some people, feelings which have often led to various forms of oppression, occasional attacks of violence, and sometimes even murder by these "gender defenders."[3] Those hostile feelings and actions are rooted in fear. In chapter 10 we will examine the development and the ramifications of this "fear syndrome" in greater detail.

We also need to be aware of the existence and influence of politically motivated, patriarchal, extremist, pseudo-Christian religious groups. These groups have strong patriarchal and anti-diversity political agendas, including regular opposition to anti-discriminatory legislative attempts for lesbian, gay, bisexual, and transgendered persons.[4] Such oppressive organizations and agendas are symptomatic of a deep-seated and pathological need to control others, characteristics that are all too frequently exhibited in our power-based culture of dominance. Christine M. Smith reminds us that we must therefore work to develop what she calls "radical responses to radical evil." We need to continually raise our awareness of the fearful, negative, hate-filled climate that these anti-diversity groups foster toward transgendered persons, and we would be wise to keep ourselves informed of the very real dangers that exist as a result.

We must also avoid tarring all social or religious conservatives with the same brush. We do a disservice to all concerned when we blindly lump any persons who disagree with us into a single negative category. Gender variant folks don't like it when people casually dismiss us as belonging to a single classification, and we have no right to do that to others in return.

We won't heal our broken relationships or ideological rifts by meeting hatred with more hatred, or violence with additional violence. Instead, we must learn to love and pray for those who struggle with such inner pain and turmoil that they feel they must antagonistically, arrogantly, or self-righteously "act out" their negativity toward others. This is not always easy, I freely admit, but God calls us to deal with people as intrinsically worthy individuals, not as members of some faceless, nonhuman category.

CRITIQUING PATRIARCHS AND POWER DYNAMICS

Rosemary Radford Ruether, a professor of theology at Garrett-Evangelical Theological Seminary, has suggested that liberating prophetic traditions contain several primary themes, including God's defense and vindication of the oppressed, a critique of the dominant systems of power, the vision of a new age to come, and a critique of the ideology that sustains the unjust order.[5] In the face of constant social, political, and religious onslaughts from those that would silence or oppress us, we who are transgendered must be continually aware of the dangers presented by those fear-based "dominant systems of power" that "sustain the unjust order."

Patriarchy presumes that it alone knows what is best for us; therefore we must do as we're told or we're somehow deviant. Carter Heyward says,

> Patriarchs know it all. It is in the character of a good patriarch not to change his mind—not to be a "wimp"—because, after all, since he is right, he has nothing to learn, no reason to change. As Margaret Mead reported on the attitude of a man who'd gone to observe the native inhabitants of a remote island: "His mind was made up, and he did not wish to have it changed by interactions with the people." Such an attitude is quintessentially patriarchal.[6]

Heyward goes on to say:

> Patriarchs do not go deeply into spiritual matters. They cannot or they would begin to tap into the divine/ human roots of their own pain and of a yearning for mutuality and connectedness. In order to avoid

this reckoning, which would spark new values, new commitments, and new life, patriarchs must stay on the surface and therefore be preoccupied with appearance.... The possibility of loving enough to set free cannot be celebrated or recognized in patriarchal relationships, precisely because the moment we set those we love free or recognize and affirm their freedom we give up our power over them and become instead their brothers, sisters, and friends.[7]

We give up our power over them.... When we actively determine to live in mutual relationship with one another, the power dynamic can be set aside. We can begin learning to live together in respect, with acceptance and appreciation for our unique human characteristics. The issue of power over others then becomes moot and is replaced with a stronger, more liberated and fulfilling way of coexisting and of being in right relationship.

LIBERATING TO AND FROM

The notion of "liberation" is multifaceted and has frequently been misunderstood by transgendered and nontransgendered persons alike. "Liberation refers to the 'for freedom Christ has set us free' of Galatians 5:1," says Carter Heyward. "Liberation is a process that has three different, interconnected aspects or levels: freedom from oppression at the social level, freedom from psychological oppression by struggling for self-fulfillment within the context of one's community, and freedom from sin."[8] If we do not consider the implications of each of these aspects then we will be unable to fully experience the richness in the amazing gift of God's liberation.

The transgendered are in need of both liberation *from* and liberation *to*. We are in need of liberation from the imposed bondage of social and religious injustices. However, it is not enough for us to simply be liberated *from* discrimination, marginalization, and oppression: we need to be liberated *to* the freedom that is found only in a personal relationship with God through Jesus Christ. Such liberation will include a freedom of gender expression for us, and this is true whether that freedom is internally or externally experienced and manifested. Liberation will also eventually involve wider acceptance, mutuality, respect, and love for the transgendered, and it will be extended from the broader community of faith, the Body of Christ. As we experience this liberation we will in turn be further emancipated to share the many gifts of our differently gendered spirits. Whether they recognize it or not, God's people and God's church desperately *need* those gifts.

STEPS TOWARD TRANSGENDER SPIRITUAL AWARENESS

I'd like to propose four very simple steps that differently gendered persons can use to help themselves become more spiritually aware. The first step is to *admit and understand that we are a minority in this world. Therefore, we need to be more aware than the average person, if only for our own protection.* Our transgendered minority status tends to put us at a disadvantage in the arena of sociocultural power, and consequently we must increase our knowledge of the world and our own human capabilities in order to protect and defend ourselves and overcome that disadvantage. Seeking answers to the hard questions will better equip us to face the dangers of hierarchical power structures, systemic injustice, destructive institutional paradigms and, especially in the case of gender variant Christians, traditional anti-transgender religious attitudes and actions. We need to understand that we are perceived as threats to the socioreligious authorities simply because we exist. As we become more aware of this unfortunate truth we can also begin to develop personal and communal strategies of survival and struggle. If we commit ourselves to this effort, both individually and collectively, we will surprise ourselves and others with our progress on a variety of levels. If we remain ignorant of our problems we are doomed to remain mired in them. The more we know, the more effective we can become on our own behalf.

The second step toward spiritual awareness for the transgendered is to *place our trust and hope in the One who created us in the "imago Dei," the divine image.* Until we can begin identifying emotionally, psychologically, physically, and spiritually with our Creator, we will be limited in achieving our full potential as valuable and capable gender variant human beings. This personal identification will inevitably create a greater sense of our own self-worth, resulting in healthier, happier, more productive, and spiritually aware differently gendered individuals. It will also allow us to develop a stronger, more beneficial relationship with our Creator, a relationship based in mutuality and trust rather than the "I'm up, you're down" ideologies of fundamentalist religion. We must learn to be partners with God in the co-creation of our gender variant lives even as we learn to depend upon God's unimaginable strength, love, and acceptance for us as individuals.

The third step is to *develop a respect and love for God, for other human beings, for all of God's creation, and for our own transgendered selves.* We are always held back from reaching our full potential if we do not move forward in life with an avid appreciation for the goodness and diversity of God's creation. This means that we may need to learn a new way of looking at the world and our place in it, especially as we relate to other people. A genuine love for others enables us to personally experience the awesome beauty of life. Then, too, we must learn to truly love ourselves as the amazing, "peculiar," and gifted gender variant people that we are. Being differently gendered gives us a remarkable lens for viewing the world. We owe it to God, to others, and to ourselves to begin seeing our world through eyes of love rather than self-hatred.

A final step toward greater transgendered spiritual awareness is to *do something good for someone else,* preferably in our transgendered persona. It's amazing how our own troubles can seem less difficult when we make an effort to help someone less fortunate than ourselves. If we find ourselves overwhelmed and paralyzed with sorrow or self-pity because of our differently gendered status, we can try volunteering at a local homeless shelter or food bank. We can visit the sick, the elderly, or prison inmates. We can donate our time and money to world hunger relief, Habitat for Humanity, AIDS research, shelters for battered women or homeless children, a lesbian/gay/bisexual/transgender Christian ministry, or any of a thousand other worthy charitable causes. Our troubles diminish considerably when we focus on others instead of our own problems. A secondary benefit of such an effort is that it will give others a new and different perspective on your worth as a transgendered individual. People will no longer be able to consider you a faceless, ominous threat, but will be inclined (and almost forced) to think of you as someone who is a real asset and a contributor.

CREATING HEALTHY TRANSGENDERED THEOLOGICAL PARADIGMS

As we've seen, a distinct and identifiable transgender theology of liberation is a necessity if we are to grow and mature in our own spiritual identities as differently gendered people of God. Our specifically transgender-based theology will undoubtedly be something of a hybrid, a synthesis formulated from, among other things, the following:

- the transgendered experience of individuals;
- the transgender community's history and culture;
- the traditions of the Christian church;

- our ongoing struggle for social, political, personal, and spiritual liberation;
- scripture;
- human reason and accumulated wisdom.

If we are to do this theological work with integrity, gender variant people must first begin the process of deconstructing our traditional (and often false) understandings about Jesus, about Christianity, and about God's historical and ongoing interaction with humanity. Only then can we be free to begin the composition of a new and relevant theology.

In addition, we must begin working out our theology as part of a communal effort. "Liberation is a personal process that takes place within and through a community," says Isasi-Díaz.[9] We who are transgendered are not isolated individuals living in a vacuum and completely untouched by what happens to our differently gendered sisters and brothers, even though it may seem that way at times. Many gender variant people can tell you firsthand that a crushing loneliness and a sense of alienation from community have often been parts of their differently gendered life experience. The story of Elijah in 1 Kings 19:9–18 tells us that even when we feel as though we are the only one in our position, God knows there are always others who are like us. Whether we recognize it or not, we are part of a global transgendered community that desperately needs a spiritual core around which to center itself and build its life.

Gender variant persons need to know that Christian clergy are willing to embrace the outcast in Jesus' name. If church leaders are not willing to reach out in love and acceptance to all people—including the differently gendered—in the name of Jesus Christ and without judgment or reservation, then we must openly question their fitness to be called ministers of the Gospel.

The clergy's evaluation of "difference" will, of course, influence how they minister to "different" persons such as the gender variant. Sadly, according to Robert Nugent and Jeannine Gramick, leaders in ministry to gay and lesbian Catholics, "the general pastoral approach . . . is to urge individuals to acknowledge their sinfulness, renounce the evil, experience a spiritual conversion, and change . . . by spiritual healing if not through psychological means. Refusal or inability to do one or the other can result in expulsion from the denomination."[10] Until this unjust and un-Christlike approach to pastoral ministry changes, differently gendered persons will remain alienated from those clergy who continue to use it.

James B. Nelson reminds us, "The *good* news is the affirmation of human equality. In one of his better moments the apostle Paul wrote, 'There is no longer Jew or Greek, there is no longer slave or free, there is no longer male or female; for all of you are one in Christ Jesus' (Gal. 3:28)."[11] *There is no longer male or female!* . . . Could this possibly mean that faith in Christ transcends the barriers of sex and gender, thus rendering each person, regardless of sexual or gender orientation, equally precious in the eyes of God?

The fact that transgendered people are forced to cope with our marginalized status, with the various forms of oppression directed against us by society, and with discrimination leveled against us by our religious institutions creates a depth of spirit that is, quite simply, unavailable to those who do not share a similar struggle. This is not to say that our sufferings are worse than those of others or that we are somehow better or more valuable than other people because of our suffering. It does mean, however, that our particular struggles can enrich our lives and our spirits. We who are differently gendered are much, much stronger than we know—we *have* to be, for we have much to endure. We must learn to lean completely on our God for strength and wisdom to persevere.

10

THE STRUGGLE FOR INCLUSION

IT IS A SOURCE of continuing sorrow and anger to me that my beloved Christianity, a religion founded upon Jesus Christ's principles of love, acceptance, mutuality, and respect for all people, has historically placed itself in a position of judgment and exclusion toward certain groups or individuals whom the institutional church has unjustly deemed less-than-whole. Women, people of color, lesbian, gay, and bisexual persons have been and continue to be victimized and marginalized as a result of this prejudicial mindset. Transgendered persons share fully in the oppressive experience of being considered outsiders and strangers and of being rendered invisible. Many gender variant people are rightfully skeptical and even bitter toward a Christianity that tolerates them only conditionally as second-class members. "Something as simple as our act to decide, think, and feel for ourselves," says Gary David Comstock, "has made the church nervous to the point of fearing that our living our lives as fully human beings threatens the foundations of family structure, the natural order, and traditional social relations."[1] Our existence and presence are a source of fear and anxiety in the church.

Much is at stake. Will the church continue to maintain its historically negative stance toward the transgendered, or will it begin to live out the intent of the Gospel with integrity, overcoming its fear of the unknown, welcoming the stranger, and lovingly affirming all people who would come to God? The primary issue for the church is therefore not one of altruism or benevolence toward the differently gendered, but rather one of justice and faithfulness to Christ's teachings regarding the wider community of the disenfranchised and powerless. This is a struggle for the church's very soul, and the ramifications for Christianity as an institution far exceed the implications for any single community or demographic group within that institution. The faith issues of gender variant people are a convenient proving ground— a gender-based litmus test, if you will—for the church's willingness to learn, to grow, and to become increasingly inclusive in its mission to be the embodiment of Christ in this world.

Is the church's table big enough to welcome all, as Christ would have it, or will male-dominated politics and internal power struggles continue to unjustly exclude the gender variant from speaking with an equal voice in the communal discourse of Christianity?

LAYERS OF FEAR

Why should the lust for religious power run so deeply in the minds and attitudes of the church's hierarchies? And why do so many individual Christians in the pews continue to accept wholeheartedly the church's historic paradigm of androcentric authority? In his book *The Courage to Teach*, Parker J. Palmer provides deep insight into the psychological reasons for these situations: he tells us that such power machinations are really all about *fear*. Fear seems to affect the lives of all human beings in some way, and that fear can occur regardless of our philosophical or ideological stance. Here's how it happens according to Palmer:

> We collaborate with the structures of separation because they promise to protect us against one of the deepest fears at the heart of being human—the fear of having a live encounter with alien "otherness,"

whether the other is a student, a colleague, a subject, or a self-dissenting voice within. We fear encounters in which the other is free to be itself, to speak its own truth, to tell us what we may not wish to hear. We want those encounters on our own terms, so that we can control their outcomes, so that they will not threaten our view of the world and self.[2]

Fear causes many religious fundamentalists to retreat into the nostalgic security of a bygone era, to grasp at any straws that offer a semblance of order in the face of their trepidation, and to loudly insist that everyone follow their example of simplistic religious answers to every question, thereby ignoring or withdrawing completely from the messy complexities of modern theological questions. In short, they want to encounter difference on their own terms so they can control the outcomes. And that frantic desire for power and control over others is a prime example of fear in action.

Of course, such a retreat from change invariably fosters a fortress mentality, a "circle the wagons" school of thought, an "us against them" approach to issues such as human diversity, represented, for instance, by the existence of the differently gendered. History is replete with examples of zealous, single-minded people who were absolutely convinced of the correctness of their exclusivist biblical literalist positions on such social issues as slavery, women's suffrage, and gender-based socioreligious roles. John Shelby Spong writes that such persons or groups

> appear to be dedicated to a simplistic view of Holy Scripture that assumes a literalness about biblical texts that has been abandoned by the academic world of scholarship for almost a century. In order to justify this mentality, they demonstrate a radical anti-intellectualism, which is marked by a defensiveness that frequently manifests itself in religious anger. They

display an overt paranoia about the causes of their increasing irrelevance. They appear to believe that there
is some organized conspiracy that is dedicated to their
destruction. They imagine these enemies to be enor-
mously powerful, and they refer to them with capital
letters, such as "The Militant Feminists," "The Gay
Lobby," or "The Secular Humanists." They see themselves as a beleaguered minority battling for the truth
of God, which they have confused with their distorted
version of truth.[3]

Peter J. Gomes calls this type of right-wing religious ideal-
ism "nostalgia with an attitude."[4] These groups believe that
they have "direct, clear, and unambiguous revelation of
God's will" on complex topics such as gender orientation.
Their punitive view on these issues interprets transgender
expression and a transgender orientation as "sinful and
prohibited by God."[5]

There are two major problems with these religious ideologies. First, they profoundly diminish the lives of their
adherents by trapping them within a faulty and incomplete
religious belief system, preventing them from experienc-
ing the full scope of God's benevolence and inclusive love
toward all humankind. Second, they generate tremendous
difficulties and spiritual obstacles for those with whom they
disagree.

If transgendered persons are ever going to gain the respect and acceptance we need and deserve, we must find
more effective ways to help the Christian community overcome its fear of anything new or different so that the church
may move into the future, trusting in the God who created us all in delightful diversity. Transcending old mindsets
rooted in xenophobia (i.e., fear of the "foreigner") will not
be an easy task—because old habits, traditional belief systems, and outmoded institutions tend to die hard—but it is
a necessary, even critical, mission if we are to progress and
become all that the church is capable of being.

FACING FEARS

It is the fear of diversity and otherness that holds us back, paralyzing us into inaction, prohibiting us from making spiritual headway and from doing the work of justice in Jesus' name. Palmer says,

> This fear of the live encounter begins . . . in the fear of diversity. As long as we inhabit a universe made homogeneous by our refusal to admit otherness, we can maintain that illusion that we possess the truth about ourselves and the world—after all, there is no "other" to challenge us! But as soon as we admit pluralism, we are forced to admit that ours is not the only standpoint, the only experience, the only way, and the truths we have built our lives on begin to feel fragile.[6]

The church fears live encounters with transgendered people, the "other," because such encounters invariably force the church to struggle with the idea that we exist in a pluralist context and that there are other ways to live. For the most part, the Christian community has a very difficult time admitting that such a struggle even exists. It's even more difficult for the church to embrace diversity and pluralism; it's too busy frenetically maintaining the fragile facade of religious homogeneity and "unity" to allow benign human difference to enter and confuse the picture.

Inevitable difficulties occur when differing human understandings collide head-on:

> If we embrace diversity, we find ourselves on the doorstep of our next fear: fear of the conflict that will ensue when divergent truths meet. . . . We fear the live encounter as a contest from which one party emerges victorious while the other leaves defeated and ashamed.[7]

This layer of fear—the fear of conflict—is essentially about our pride. We can't easily abide the idea of losing (or even of changing) because to do so would be to admit defeat. After all, if we have to change then that must mean we were somehow wrong, and a good patriarch can't admit *that*, so we avoid the hard confrontations. This avoidance tactic is used by both institutions and individuals, which explains why the church and its members so often refuse to take risks and bold stands for justice, timidly tap-dancing around critical issues of social and spiritual significance while God's disenfranchised people continue to twist slowly in the wind.

Next, says Palmer, "if we peel back our fear of conflict, we find a third layer of fear, the fear of losing identity. Many of us are so deeply identified with our ideas that when we have a competitive encounter, we risk losing more than the debate: we risk losing our sense of self."[8] People who are insecure in themselves or in their faith simply can't handle that sort of risk. They have too much invested in their rigid system of belief and its indisputable answers, and the idea of change is just too frightening for them.

The church is genuinely afraid of losing its historical (though distorted and inflated) sense of self, particularly in the area of androcentric, hierarchical control. We who are differently gendered make perfect scapegoats for that fear. The transgendered are, after all, human mirrors, holding society's gender roles and expectations up for examination and possible alteration, and those in power do not like that idea one bit. Honest reassessment might lead to a lessening of their established power base. In transgendered persons the religious authorities see all that they dread—transformation, otherness, new ideas, different ways of being and presenting oneself, a potential transfer of sociospiritual power to the individual and away from the dominant establishment, the discarding of old, outmoded, ineffective religious concepts and the embracing of the new—and so the gender variant are fervently portrayed as the enemies of everything that the powerful institution of Christianity holds dear.

Thankfully, however, there are increasing numbers of people of all gender and sexual orientations within the Christian community who recognize the exclusivist allegations for what they are: unjust, unfair, discriminatory, un-Christlike, prejudicial, heretical, and totally antithetical to the inclusive intent and purpose of the Gospel. These compassionate, enlightened persons understand that faith, ethics, and strong values are not the franchise of religious ultraconservatives. Justice-loving people are beginning to make their voices heard, and, despite efforts to silence them or drown them out, they are determined to make a difference in Jesus' name. Differently gendered Christians, of course, have the responsibility to add our voices to this call for justice and transformative action on our own behalf.

We have one last layer of fear to confront:

> If we embrace the promise of diversity, of creative conflict, and of "losing" in order to "win," we still face one final fear—the fear that a live encounter with otherness will change or even compel us to change our lives. This is not paranoia: the world really *is* out to get us! Otherness, taken seriously, always invites transformation, calling us not only to new facts and theories and values but also to new ways of living our lives—and that is the most daunting threat of all.[9]

Fear, not other human beings, is our enemy. It is what keeps the extremist religious right imprisoned within their cages of mandatory pseudo-religious homogeneity, false "unity," theological exclusivity, and blind adherence to an outmoded, medieval ethos of gender and human relationships. The transformation of these soul-killing paradigms within the church is essential if we are to achieve a place at the table of Christian equality for all those who may be "different."

AN INCLUSIVE ALTERNATIVE
TO HIERARCHY

Everyone wants to be included, to belong. It's human nature. We were designed by God to be social creatures, living
together in community. That's why inclusive language in the
church is such a vital issue: it represents the symbolic need
for every person to belong, to be included, to be spoken
of as though they matter. The struggle for inclusive language—theological words and ideas that include *everyone,*
not just white, heterosexual, nontransgendered males—in
the church continues to be long and difficult, but the reasons
for that struggle are powerful and undeniable. Inclusive language is a conscious effort to set aside the androcentric,
patriarchal manner of speaking about God while endeav-
oring to use words, images, metaphors, and concepts that
include all of humanity in their fullness and their implications. Transgendered persons should be especially aware of
the importance of fostering and even insisting upon a lexi-
con of inclusivity within the Body of Christ, for without the
common adoption of such language we are doomed to remain forever trapped in a male-dominated and hierarchical
theological morass.

Carolyn Henninger Oehler, theologian and executive di-
rector of the Scarritt-Bennett Center in Nashville, writes
eloquently of the traditionally exclusive model of dominance and subordination within the church: "Moving
[toward a] justice based, inclusive spirituality means leav-
ing behind language and imagery that foster dominance
metaphors for reality and embracing those that 'affirm reciprocity in action.' "[10] We need words and images that can
help us claim the role of co-creator in our relationship
to God and to other persons. Barbara Anne Keely, associate professor of Christian Education at United Theological
Seminary of the Twin Cities, reminds us of our need to
"understand the power of language to shape our imagi-
nation and our images of God. *God is not "he," God is*

"God," and the language we use to talk about God shapes our understanding of God and what it means for us— female and male—to be made in the image of God."[11] These theological distinctions and linguistic nuances are especially critical for differently gendered persons, who find ourselves living on the margins of society's gender expectations for both males and females. Henninger Oehler continues:

> We have ample evidence of the inadequacy of and damage done by male-dominated language and under-standing. In the traditional hierarchy of dominance, God is viewed as Lord, King, all-powerful, transcen-dent, demanding human submission, and fostering a sense of human powerlessness. Coming next in the hierarchy, males assume the role of dominance over those beneath them.[12]

To permit a "nonmale" to assume a position of authority in the church is to go against the church's established cus-toms and the traditional religious culture of androcentric theological interpretation. Allowing a designated "other" to openly achieve full, active membership and an equal voice within the Body of Christ effectively opposes the his-toric institutional structure, which explains the difficulty that transgendered people have historically faced within the church itself. Henninger Oehler states further:

> In this hierarchy, so-called generic language is com-mon, with the male noun or pronoun used to represent all persons. The users of this language may not intend to be exclusive, but the effect nevertheless is to deny [the] separate identity and power [of non-males], both linguistically and in relationships. Dominating white male imagery and language serve to enforce subordi-nation of other groups as well—by race, by class, by sexual orientation.[13]

We need to struggle against the tyranny of exclusively male theological language because our concepts of God and of each other need to be larger and more comprehensive than that. Solely masculine God-language attempts to put God in a box. Of course, patriarchal fundamentalists like that idea; by keeping God in a box they can more readily monitor theological thought and control the behavior of others, keeping them in check. We owe it to our Creator and ourselves to move beyond the idolatry of an androcentric vocabulary into the fullness of inclusivity as expressed in our language, our religio-spiritual imagery, and our ideas of God.

Henninger Oehler's words remind us that our theological mindsets are inevitably shaped by the words and images that we use in our relationships with God and with each other. As differently gendered persons, we must be aware of the dangers of allowing exclusively male terminology and imagery to structure the ways we think and act within those relationships. We do a disservice to everyone when we continue to allow patriarchy and androcentrism to control how we speak in our spirituality and how we express our self-understanding as people of God. Ada María Isasi-Díaz tells us, "We use *kin-dom* instead of *kingdom* because the latter is obviously a sexist word that presumes God is male; elitist—that is why we do not use *reign. Kin-dom* makes it clear that when the fullness of God becomes a reality, we will all be sisters and brothers—kin to each other."[14]

The lives of differently gendered persons are constant reminders to the world that there are, quite simply, other ways to be. Transgendered Christians are only now beginning to recognize our significant numbers and our manifold contributions to the life of the church. Those who would deny us full, complete membership in the Body of Christ should know that *we will not be denied forever, and our patience grows increasingly thin.* We will no longer cooperate as we are forced to the floor, and we will not be satisfied with licking at the crumbs that fall from the table of Christian communion. Second-class citizenship in the Christian community of faith is no longer an option. We're beginning to recognize that we don't have to stand submissively and quietly by as the powers that be attempt to force us into invisibility, denying our right to full communion and egalitarian status at God's banquet table.

We are gender variant human beings who are fearfully and wonderfully created in the image of God like every other person. That truth automatically confers upon us the right to complete an unabridged membership in the Body of Christ if we so desire. However, with that God-given right comes a corresponding responsibility: difficult and frightening though it may be, Christians who are transgendered *must* begin to come out to the church. We must begin letting others know who we are, making our presence felt and our spiritual needs known even as we assert our rightful place in the forefront of the struggle for liberating transformation. Justice-loving Christians of all ages, colors, abilities, and sexual and gender orientations must join together to transform the church at the root so it can become the totally welcoming, loving, respectful, and inclusive institution that our God always intended it to be.

11

THE NEEDS AND HOPES OF TRANSGENDERED CHRISTIANS

EVEN WHEN I was very young, perhaps only two or three, I knew I was different. I sensed it, actually, more than I understood it. It seems that many, if not most, who are transgendered learn about our difference early in life. Though we didn't invite it—and though it may not always be welcomed—the difference is always there, subtly or perhaps not-so-subtly making its presence felt and informing our gender variant existence in any number of ways.

There is a strange, almost morbid fascination, a kind of secret compulsion, that seems to focus on transgendered persons. Interestingly enough, this is especially true in traditionally conservative social institutions like the Christian church. We who are differently gendered tend to repulse and anger some people, it is true, but we also manage to intrigue and interest them. People can't seem to help wondering what we're like, what we do, why we do it, what kind of people we are, and why we even exist in the first place. Part of the allure of transgenderism is that we refuse to be confined by the conventional social rules of gender. We transgress the culture's gender boundaries, and therefore we represent potential anarchy and chaos to some. To others we represent a pioneering spirit, a delightfully embodied freedom from society's imposed appearance and behavior regulations. We create confusion and irritability in some people, curiosity and attraction in others.

Sometimes all of these coexist in the same person at the same time.

Gender variant people are inexorably, inexplicably drawn to reject, ignore, or move beyond the typical masculine or feminine gender expectations for one's biological sex that society has decreed. That nonconformity can reveal itself in different ways, but such manifestations usually take the form of a certain type of gender presentation. And because those varying and stylized gender presentations can fly in the face of society's rigid but arbitrarily determined gender paradigms, we transgendered folk make some people angry. They're angry because we defy the rules. They're angry because we cross over the clear-cut boundaries of gender that help people form their tidy views of the world, creating confusion and psychological discomfort. Some people are angry and frustrated because they secretly wish they could do what we do—but can't, or won't. Some are angry because they believe our existence is a threat to their religious beliefs or to their base of social power; they fear us, and their fear translates into animosity and hatred. Some are angry because we excite them sexually and they cannot understand why. Some are angry because they simply don't like anything or anyone that's different. And some are angry because gender variant persons remind them of a deep, dark, unexplored part of themselves that they'd like to ignore or pretend doesn't exist.

Most people know relatively little about the real lives of transgendered persons. We are perceived as alien, other, and mysterious. Instead of helping to disseminate truthful, realistic information about the benign nature of transgenderism, the mass media have generally served only to complicate, sensationalize, and confuse the issue. The spiritual concerns of the differently gendered, especially as they pertain to the institutional Christian church, are a legitimate issue that deserves to be addressed. We need clarity and insight, not confusion and hearsay, to effectively confront that issue.

WHY THIS STRUGGLE IS NECESSARY

A few years ago I wrote a little booklet called *The Cross and the Crossdresser: Personal Reflections on Crossdressing from a Christian Perspective.* I later heard from a transgendered person, a crossdresser named Linda.[1] Her letter reads as follows:

I could no longer deal with the overpowering guilt and shame that my religion made me feel because I need to crossdress. I just couldn't stand it anymore. I was sitting in a chair in my living room with a gun in one hand and your book in the other, and I was planning to kill myself because my pain was so intense. I began to read, and when I read your words about God's love and acceptance for all people I began to weep. I cried and prayed for a while and then kept on reading. Finally, I put the gun down so I could turn the pages more easily. I finished the book and sat there for a long time, thinking about what I'd just read. Then I made a decision to trust in God's love rather than my religion or my pastor. God knows that I'm a crossdresser, and I decided that God really does love me, dresses, heels, makeup, and all. I unloaded the gun and put it away. I'm much more at peace, though very sad about what's happened to me in the past. I'm now going to look for a new church, one that will accept me as I am, and try to live a happy life in Jesus Christ.

That letter from the very edge of the abyss continues to haunt me. It reminds me of all the struggle, rejection, and heartache that so many of our Christian transgendered sisters and brothers experience every day. Linda's situation is not an atypical example of what the institutional Christian church has done and continues to do to differently gendered people. As we have seen, suicide rates, poverty, drug abuse, and alcoholism within the transgender community are several times the national average, and this can be attributed in large part to the lack of support and acceptance shown by society and its institutions, including the church. Sidney G. Hall III writes

> There is so much pain that has been shared. . . . We hear the stories and we meet the people behind the stories. . . . We know the people who sit in silent pain in the pews Sunday after Sunday. . . . Many of these are people who wonder if they are absolutely alone in this world and have not found a way to see themselves as God's included. They have not been fortunate enough to encounter others who see the face of Christ in their face.[2]

People who fear difference seek predictability, safety, and quite often religious homogeneity. A few hundred years ago people in Salem, Massachusetts, accused their neighbors of being witches and monsters. They murdered them by hanging, stoning, drowning, or burning them at the stake because they feared what they didn't understand. Their religion had taught them that it was permissible, perhaps even advisable, to kill people who were different.

The thought process is something like the following: "Inclusivity? Sure, we're inclusive. We love everybody here at our church. Just don't ask me to sit next to weirdos who are different from me. It makes me feel a little strange to see them there. I don't like feeling uneasy or being challenged in church. You know, I come here to feel relaxed and comfortable with other people who are just like me. Besides, anybody who's different is probably really weird and maybe even dangerous."

HONESTY AND HERESY

A sexist church, a homophobic church, a heterosexist church, a racist church, a misogynistic church, and a transgenderphobic church is not worthy of the name "Christian." Gays, lesbians, bisexuals, and transgendered people have been part of the church for as long as Christianity has been around, although the powers that be are extremely loath to admit it.

Gender variant people express our differently gendered selves externally because we've always been transgendered internally. Whether we've always been consciously aware of it or not is another matter, but many of us knew at an early age. Most of us who are transgendered did not know the word "deviant" when we were small, but we quickly learned words such as "bad," "sissy," "faggot," and "dyke." Our churches, schools, and other social institutions made very sure of that. Our external gender presentation is simply an honest expression of what's going on internally. The church would prefer that we be invisible, deceitful, and dishonest about who and what we are in the name of its cherished social order and "unity." Thought and behavior control is exercised so that everyone will maintain a façade of gender correctness "as God has so obviously ordained."

The refusal of the Body of Christ to address the spiritual presence and concerns of differently gendered people—to welcome us and to stand up in love for an unpopular and misunderstood minority group—is an affront to the very God who created human beings in such amazing diversity. The dictionary defines heresy as "religious opinion or doctrine at variance with the orthodox or accepted doctrine." Is it not "at variance with the orthodox or accepted doctrine" to reject or abandon the disenfranchised and the dispossessed, the people that Jesus came to love and save with his message of inclusivity and acceptance? Whenever the church turns its back on the community of the oppressed, ignores the sufferings of others, or refuses to act in the cause of justice, that's heresy. Whenever those who are supposed to represent Jesus turn a blind eye and a deaf ear to the spiritual gifts of transgendered people, and when those differently gendered spiritual gifts are rejected by the church because of unfounded fear, bigotry, and prejudice, that's heresy. And whenever the legitimate spiritual needs and concerns of gender variant persons are dismissed as trivial, that's heresy. It flies in the face of all that Jesus taught and stood for, and it's the absolute antithesis of the good news of Christ's liberating Gospel for all people.

In some ways the church is fast becoming an archaic institution, an anachronistic dinosaur that refuses to address or confront its problems in meaningful ways and that has little relevance to the problems and concerns of today. Christianity as a whole is losing members in droves because thinking people are realizing the futility of an outmoded belief system that demands blind, unquestioning adherence to a medieval worldview and to an ethos that ineptly attempts to define and regulate the complex social, sexual, and gendered relationships of human beings. We need to generate new and progressive ways to enliven hearts while engaging the minds and quickening the spirits of church members. The bleak alternative is a slow, downward death-spiral.

Church members are voting with their feet, and their increased departures from the community of faith are strong indications of the church's lack of ability to effectively confront, discuss, and take action upon the pressing issues of our times. The important matters that directly affect people's lives should always be our focus for ministry, yet Christianity's institutional mindset is far too often rooted in an idolatrous and spiritually inept paradigm that takes the Bible literally, depending upon simplistic theological answers to complex, modern-day concerns. Conservative-evangelical churches, however, are increasing their memberships and influence because people are seeking spiritual reassurance, safety, and comfort in this rapidly changing world. Fundamentalist churches offer pat answers and security for religious seekers.

RESPONDING TO NEEDS

In order to be faithful to the Gospel, congregations need to be responsive to the complex issues of the day, including those of gender and sexuality.

Some have made the argument, "We don't have any transgendered people in our church. Why should we go out of our way to do anything at all when there aren't any of them here in the first place?"

I would respond: How do you know there aren't any transgendered people in your church? Have you tried to find out? Have you worked to create a climate of welcome and affirmation so that any closeted transgendered people could safely "come out" and be open in your congregation? If not, how can you expect differently gendered persons to make themselves known in a potentially hostile religious environment?

A pastor friend once told me of visiting a large mainstream denominational church that had made no accommodations for the physically disabled—no ramps for wheelchairs, no elevators, no ASL signers, etc. He asked a member of the congregation about this and was told, "Oh, we don't have any disabled people like that in our church." Is it any wonder why? If you were physically disabled, would you attend that church? If we don't take visible and sensible steps to make people feel welcomed, they aren't going to be a viable part of our faith communities.

What are the real spiritual needs of transgendered persons? Those needs take the following forms:

The need for education and dialogue. There is a critical need for education in society and in the church regarding transgenderism. The church needs to:

- raise the general awareness of Christians about the existence, nature, and spiritual needs of gender variant persons;

- create a body of reliable information on transgenderism that is available for in-depth study;

- allow questions to be raised, concerns to be voiced, and fears to be addressed so that ignorance can be dispelled and bridges of respect can be built;

- demonstrate that Christians genuinely recognize and care about injustice in all its forms and are willing to do something about it;

- work swiftly and persistently toward developing effective outreach ministries, sharing the accepting, affirming love of God with the transgendered and with other gender/sexual minority communities;

- create a welcoming spiritual environment in which differently gendered people are respected, affirmed, and appreciated as valuable contributors to the life of the church.

We need education for both the church and the transgender community so we can more readily confront the systemic and radical evil of society and its institutions. That evil is often cleverly disguised by the silver-tongued rhetoric and the glib euphemisms of its perpetrators, but it takes such forms as racism, misogyny, ableism, homophobia, ageism, heterosexism, religious arrogance, and transgenderphobia. If we can become increasingly aware of evil's presence and varied manifestations then we can begin to act boldly and decisively against it.

Additionally, the more we know about each other's lives and experiences the more we can act responsibly and lovingly toward each other. Familiarization and factual, nonsensationalistic information can be a tremendous help in overcoming the barriers to authentic understanding and meaningful communication.

We must speak intentionally about what a differently gendered presence means for the church and for society, and we must enter that conversation in a spirit of cooperation and respect so that we may genuinely learn from each other. As Gerald Mallon says,

> Part of the way in which our society maintains stereotypes and negative attitudes about transgendered persons is by refusing to consider them as a legitimate

topic for discussion in our homes or...institutions. Such silence allows stereotypes to be maintained because positive images that reflect the reality of transgendered persons have been extremely limited in the media.[3]

Honest, open dialogue will engender questions, and questions will stimulate reflection and a greater overall awareness. This in turn will lead to a lessening of fear and will eventually allow for acceptance and affirmation.

The need for love. Like all humans, differently gendered persons need pure, simple, and unconditional love. I'm speaking of *agape* love, love without strings or conditions, love that can transcend superficial differences and embrace the common humanity that we share, love that creates inclusive community. The Christian community must reach out with the love of our Creator to the differently gendered so that healing and reconciliation can take place, and gender variant persons must respond in good faith.

The need for respect, acceptance, and encouragement. We need a place at the table and an equal voice in the dialogue, and it's in the church's own best interests to provide them. I understand that people may be squeamish and uncertain about this, especially at first. I know it may initially seem strange to see gender variant people openly taking part in the worship and daily activities of a local congregation or faith community, but if the church is to fulfill its God-given mandate to be just and inclusive, then such occurrences must become regular. The initial novelty will quickly subside and differently gendered persons will no longer suffer religious stigma or unhealthy scrutiny at the hands of mainstream Christianity. Affirmation, respect, and acceptance will become the norm rather than the exception, and we can then celebrate our differences as well as our common humanity.

The need for social activism on behalf of transgender rights. Think of how people like Jesus, Joan of Arc, Mahatma Gandhi, and Martin Luther King Jr. changed human understanding by taking strong ethical and spiritually based stands for what they knew to be true. They paid for those stands with their lives, but the world is better because they did so.

Differently gendered people don't want or need *special* rights in society, but we do expect the same civil and human rights that others enjoy, without fear of reprisal or retribution, as we attempt to contribute to the world and live our lives with dignity and purpose. To date, says Wendell Glenn,

> no one has actually devised programs for third gender populations to advance themselves socially, economically, or politically. Although there are some unique needs with this population, most of us want the same things that everyone else wants—respect, a decent living wage, affordable housing, adequate health care, and people around us who really care about us. We have yet to see a legislative body or social program with the mandate and the agenda to adequately serve this population.[4]

The church has a golden opportunity to demonstrate the love of God by taking the lead in spiritual, social, and legal advocacy for the gender variant community.

BLESSINGS WITH A PRICE

Differently gendered believers are isolated in both their identity communities. In the institutional church we are castigated in virtually every denomination. Outside the religious communities, on the other hand, many in the (generally bitter) gender variant community see differently gendered activist believers as dupes or masochists engaged in a neurotic and meaningless struggle.[5] However, transgendered Christian activists are not latter-day Don or Doña Quixotes unrealistically tilting at windmills, chasing impossible dreams, or pursuing noble but already lost causes. One blessed day we *will* see full inclusion and acceptance for the differently gendered within the church, and this will happen not because we are smarter than the opposition or because we're better tacticians or harder workers. Acceptance and inclusion will occur simply because our cause is just and because God is our Liberator.

We can only imagine what might have happened if Mahatma Gandhi had said, "The British are just too powerful. We can't win against the ruling might of the British Empire, so we may as well give up and go home." What if Dr. Martin Luther King Jr. had decided that the odds confronting the African-American civil rights movement of the 1950s and 1960s were simply too great to challenge? He could have easily said, "The forces of bigotry and prejudice are overwhelming. They'll crush us. We'll never achieve our objective. They won't let us. We might as well not even make the effort. We'd be better off learning to accept our demeaning, second-class status and not making waves." And what if Jesus Christ had decided, "I'm afraid to die. I don't want to suffer on that cross. Listen, Abba, maybe you'd better find someone else to do this. I think I'll just go home and stop preaching about justice and love so the authorities will leave me alone." The obstacles might sometimes appear insurmountable for gender variant Christians, too, but we must unceasingly do the work of liberation on our own behalf, trusting that our God, the source of our strength and hope, will provide what we need to see us through the struggle.

In *He Is Risen,* Thomas Merton writes,

> True encounter with Christ liberates something in us, a power we did not know we had, a hope, a capacity for life, a resilience, an ability to bounce back when we thought we were completely defeated, a capacity to grow and change, a power of creative transformation.
>
> A Christian's entire life is changed by the presence of the Risen Christ.

For the Christian there is no defeat, because Christ is risen and lives in us, and Christ has overcome all that seeks to destroy us or to block our human and spiritual growth.[6]

Merton understands that spiritual liberation is inextricably connected to a personal encounter with the person of Jesus Christ. That encounter with Christ is especially important for those of us who are "different." Through this encounter we are given hope, spiritual empowerment, and ultimate freedom.

"Some blessings don't come easily," says Patrick Gambill-Read. "Some blessings carry a price. Some blessings leave you walking differently for the rest of your days, and give you a whole new name. Some blessings spill over into the actions of those around you, and those who come after you."[7] Transgendered persons have the potential to be that kind of blessing to the Christian church.

However, there is a caveat: all Christians should be aware that welcoming people who are "different" into our churches will change the church. When gender variant persons become a viable, visible part of a faith community, that community will be challenged and changed. A new beginning will take place; agendas and awarenesses will alter; spiritual growth and intellectual and emotional stretching will occur, sometimes painfully; relationships will be affected; previously unimagined questions and concerns will arise; old, outmoded beliefs will be reassessed; new opportunities for ministry will be encountered. Our children and adults will learn about the beauty and goodness of difference, and our churches and people will be stronger and better for all of that.

The struggle for transgender liberation looms large and imposing before us. We must confront evil in its various incarnations, and we must deal with false ideologies and arrogant, bullying tactics. We will sometimes become discouraged at our apparent lack of progress, but with God's help we will move forward into a new era when we will see the liberating, inclusive love of Christ revealed in new and astonishing ways. May we each come to know that extraordinary salvific and life-giving love for ourselves. "Stand fast therefore in the liberty wherewith Christ hath made us free," says Paul, "and be not entangled again with the yoke of bondage" (Gal. 5:1).

NOTES

Foreword

1. Dietrich Bonhoeffer, *Life Together,* trans. John W. Doberstein (New York: Harper & Brothers, 1954), 97f.

Preface

1. Thomas Merton, *He Is Risen* (Niles, Ill.: Argus Communications, 1975), 22.

2. Peter J. Gomes, *The Good Book: Reading the Bible with Mind and Heart* (New York: Avon Books, 1998), 162.

3. Paraphrased from John Shelby Spong, *Here I Stand: My Struggle for a Christianity of Integrity, Love, and Equality* (San Francisco: HarperSanFrancisco), 135.

4. Michael Ray and Rochelle Myers, *Creativity in Business* (New York: Doubleday, 1988), 9.

Chapter 1: On Being Different

1. Christian Burgess, "Internal and External Stress Factors Associated with the Identity Development of Transgendered Youth," *Social Services with Transgendered Youth,* ed. Gerald P. Mallon (New York: Harrington Park Press, 1999), 46.

2. Don Miguel Ruiz, *The Four Agreements* (San Rafael, Calif.: Amber-Allen Publishing, 1997), 11.

3. Leonardo Boff and Clodovis Boff, "A Concise History of Liberation Theology," *Introducing Liberation Theology* (Maryknoll, N.Y.: Orbis Books, 1987); also available at www.landreform.org/boff2.htm.

4. Wendell D. Glenn, "Reflections of an Emerging Male-to-Female Transgendered Consciousness," in *Social Services with Transgendered Youth,* ed. Gerald D. Mallon (New York: Harrington Park Press, 1999), 84.

5. Ibid, 14.

6. Carter Heyward, *Touching Our Strength* (San Francisco: HarperSanFrancisco, 1989), 126.

7. Kate Bornstein, *Gender Outlaw* (New York: Vintage Books, 1994), 81.

Chapter 2: Confronting the Complexities of Difference and Faith

1. Michael J. O'Connell, "Counterpoint," *Minneapolis Star Tribune*, June 22, 1997, A8.
2. Eleazar Fernandez, *Toward a Theology of Struggle* (Maryknoll, N.Y.: Orbis Books, 1994), 68.
3. Ibid, 61.
4. Philip Wogaman, quoted by Laurie Goodstein, "In Depth: Preaching to the President," *Minneapolis Star Tribune*, March 2, 1998, A12.
5. Pat Califia, *Sex Changes: The Politics of Transgenderism* (San Francisco: Cleis Press, 1997), 2.
6. Susan Hill Lindley, *You Have Stept Out of Your Place* (Louisville: Westminster/John Knox Press, 1996), x.
7. Leslie Feinberg, *Transgender Warriors: Making History from Joan of Arc to RuPaul* (Boston: Beacon Press, 1996), 68.
8. Richard Green, *Sexual Identity Conflict in Children and Adults* (New York: Bantam Books, 1974), 6.
9. Look up the name "Tyra Hunter" on the Internet to learn more about the tragic and unnecessary death of a transgendered woman. Emergency medical technicians allowed Hunter to bleed to death of internal injuries when they discovered that she was gender variant.

Chapter 3: Clarifying Gender and Transgender

1. Gordene O. MacKenzie, *Transgender Nation* (Bowling Green, Ky.: Bowling Green State University Popular Press, 1994), 103.
2. Gerald P. Mallon, ed., "Knowledge for Practice with Transgendered Persons," in *Social Services with Transgendered Youth*, ed. Gerald P. Mallon (New York: Harrington Park Press, 1999), 6.
3. Ibid.
4. Ken Cooper, "Practice with Transgendered Youth and Their Families," *Social Services with Transgendered Youth*, ed. Gerald P. Mallon (New York: Harrington Park Press, 1999), 113.
5. MacKenzie, *Transgender Nation*, 4.
6. Kate Bornstein, *My Gender Workbook* (New York: Routledge, 1998), 26.
7. John Money, *Gay, Straight and In-Between: The Sexology of Erotic Orientation* (New York: Oxford University Press, 1988).
8. Patrick Gambill-Read, "Peniel, Pronouns, and Pookas," sermon given at a chapel service of United Theological Seminary of the Twin Cities, September 21, 2000, 4–5; used with permission.
9. J. J. Allen, *The Man in the Red Velvet Dress* (New York: Carol Publishing Group, 1996), 126.

10. Mallon, "Knowledge for Practice with Transgendered Persons," 14.

11. Cooper, "Practice with Transgendered Youth and Their Families," 114.

12. Ibid., 112.

13. Ibid.

14. Research indicates that there are potentially many genders; some societies certainly have more than two. However, for the sake of simplicity we will primarily confine our discussion here to the predominant binary gender categories in North American culture: masculine and feminine.

15. IFGE is the largest and best-known transgender organization in the world today and is actively involved in support and educational outreach. This organization can be reached at IFGE, P.O. Box 229, Waltham, MA 02154; phone: 617-894-8340; E-mail: IFGE@world.std.com.

16. Richard F. Docter, *Transvestites and Transsexuals: Toward a Theory of Cross-Gender Behavior* (New York: Plenum Press, 1990), 24–34.

17. Anne Fausto-Sterling, "The Five Sexes, Revisited," originally published by the New York Academy of Sciences, July/August 2000, and available online at http://www.nyas.org/membersonly/sciences/sci0007/fausto.html.

18. Ibid.

19. Ibid.

20. These are "thin" definitions, according to ethnologist Clifford Geertz. Geertz's concept will be discussed further below.

21. For a more comprehensive approach to the historical aspects of transgenderism, I refer the reader to Leslie Feinberg's wonderful book, *Transgender Warriors: Making History from Joan of Arc to RuPaul* (Boston: Beacon Press, 1996). Feinberg has written an extremely interesting, and often moving work that illuminates the rich, interesting and socially significant history of transgendered people.

22. Kathryn J. Helms, "Religion and Cross-Gender Behavior: Wellspring of Hope or Swamp of Despair?" *Gender Blending,* ed. Bonnie Bullough, Vern Bullough, and James Elias (Amherst, N.Y.: Prometheus Books, 1997), 400–401.

23. Rita Nakashima Brock, *Journeys by Heart: A Christology of Erotic Power* (New York: Crossroad, 1998), 7.

Chapter 4: Opening Pandora's Box

1. Mary Douglas, *Purity and Danger: An Analysis of Concepts of Pollution and Taboo* (New York: Praeger, 1966), 4.

2. Marjorie Garber, *Vested Interests: Cross-dressing and Cultural Anxiety* (New York: Routledge, 1992).

3. J. J. Allen, "The Man in the Red Velvet Dress," *Transgender Tapestry* 76 (Waltham, Mass.: IFGE, 1996), D3.

4. Ibid., D18.

5. Eleazar Fernandez, *Toward a Theology of Struggle* (Maryknoll, N.Y.: Orbis, 1994), 1.

6. Ibid.

7. Ken Cooper, "Practice with Transgendered Youth and Their Families," *Social Services with Transgendered Youth,* ed. Gerald P. Mallon (New York: Harrington Park Press, 1999), 128.

8. Kate Bornstein, *Gender Outlaw* (New York: Vintage Books 1994), 83.

9. Christine M. Smith, *Weaving the Sermon: Preaching in a Feminist Perspective* (Louisville: Westminster/John Knox Press, 1989), 19. I am grateful to Chris Smith for her personal encouragement and her wonderful teaching. Her friendship and deep commitment to her beliefs have been inspirational gifts to me, and I respect her tremendously.

10. James H. Cone, *God of the Oppressed* (New York: Seabury Press, 1975), 37.

11. Stephen Breck Reid, *Experience and Tradition* (Nashville: Abingdon Press, 1990), 83.

Chapter 5: Addressing Concerns about Transgenderism

1. For further information regarding the fascinating history of transgendered people, I again refer the reader to Leslie Feinberg, *Transgender Warriors: Making History from Joan of Arc to RuPaul* (Boston: Beacon Press, 1996).

2. Ken Cooper, "Practice with Transgendered Youth and Their Families," *Social Services with Transgendered Youth,* ed. Gerald P. Mallon (New York: Harrington Park Press, 1999), 114.

3. Ibid., 52.

4. Ibid., 51.

5. Leslie Feinberg, *Stone Butch Blues* (Ithaca, N.Y.: Firebrand Books, 1993), 13, 19.

6. Joshua Gamson, *Freaks Talk Back: Tabloid Talk Shows and Sexual Nonconformity* (Chicago: University of Chicago Press, 1998), 141.

7. Riki Anne Wilchins, *Read My Lips* (Ithaca, N.Y.: Firebrand Books, 1997), 25.

8. According to the Book of Genesis, God created human individuals well before the establishment of the first human and social institutions. This should perhaps tell us something about the way God views the worth of individual persons as opposed to that of institutions in general.

Institutions are certainly not unimportant or irrelevant for society, but they do need to be kept in perspective. Our institutions should always exist to be the servants, not the oppressors, of human beings.

9. John Shelby Spong, *Here I Stand: My Struggle for a Christianity of Integrity, Love, and Equality* (San Francisco: HarperSanFrancisco, 2000), 102.

10. Beverly Wildung Harrison, *Making the Connections: Essays in Feminist Social Ethics* (Boston: Beacon Press, 1985), 18.

Chapter 6: "Compassionate Condemnation"

1. John Whalen, congregation co-president, St. Paul-Reformation Lutheran Church, *Soaring with Wingspan*, newsletter of Wingspan Ministries, December 10, 2000, 1.

2. Carter Heyward, *Saving Jesus from Those Who Are Right* (Minneapolis: Fortress Press, 1999), xvi.

3. The stories of transgendered persons in this chapter, with the exception of Jade C. Devlin's story, are retellings in which names and details have been changed to protect the confidentiality of the individuals concerned.

4. The child molestation myth rears its ugly head again! The prevalence and persistence of this blatant, insidious falsehood in our culture is both amazing and disgusting.

5. Purging is a relatively common experience among crossdressers who are consumed with guilt about their behavior. It involves throwing away the differently gendered clothing in an effort to rid oneself of the desire to crossdress. However, this method of denial almost never works. The usual result is an eventual return to the crossdressing behavior, only now the person has to buy new clothes and spend more money to replace those things that were discarded. It would be far better for the person to work toward self-acceptance, finding a way to integrate those transgender desires into the overall fabric of her or his life instead of being immersed in guilt and shame over an internal desire that, in reality, harms no one.

6. Heyward, *Saving Jesus from Those Who Are Right*, xiv.

7. Adapted from Rik Isensee, *Reclaiming Your Life* (Los Angeles: Alyson Books, 1997), 9.

8. Gary David Comstock, "Aliens in the Promised Land?: keynote address for the 1986 National Gathering of the United Church of Christ's Coalition for Lesbian/Gay Concerns," *Homosexuality and Religion*, ed. Richard Hasbany (New York: Harrington Park Press, 1989), 134.

9. Jim May, excerpts from "Christ, Not Christianity," *Union Life*, May 1997.

10. Michael Ray and Rochelle Myers, *Creativity in Business* (New York: Doubleday, 1988), 9.

11. Marcus J. Borg, *The God We Never Knew: Beyond Dogmatic Religion to a More Authentic Contemporary Faith* (San Francisco: HarperSanFrancisco, 1997), 150.

12. John Bowman as quoted by Stephen Breck Reid, *Experience and Tradition* (Nashville: Abingdon Press, 1990), 123–24.

13. Stephen Beers, from an editorial in *Focus Point* 7, no. 17, Issue 278, Minneapolis (October 6, 1999): 8.

14. The story is recounted here with the permission of Jade Devlin.

Chapter 7: A Transgendered Christian Church?

1. J. J. Allen, *The Man in the Red Velvet Dress* (New York: Carol Publishing Group, 1996), 127.

2. Read Virginia Ramey Mollenkott's *The Divine Feminine: The Biblical Imagery of God as Female* (New York: Crossroad, 1983) for further information about the many "other" images of God contained in scripture.

3. John Shelby Spong, *Here I Stand: My Struggle for a Christianity of Integrity, Love, and Equality* (San Francisco: HarperSanFrancisco, 2000), 254–55.

4. Ibid., 408.

5. Adapted from a text by Barbara Jean Jason, a writer active in an online transgendered Christian fellowship.

6. I am indebted to my friend Jade C. Devlin for these clarifying and useful insights into the behavioral characteristics of Jesus.

7. Eleanor McLaughlin, "Feminist Christologies: Re-Dressing the Tradition," in *Reconstructing the Christ Symbol*, ed. Maryanne Stevens (New York: Paulist Press, 1993), 134.

8. Marcus J. Borg, *The God We Never Knew: Beyond Dogmatic Religion to a More Authentic Contemporary Faith* (San Francisco: HarperSanFrancisco, 1997), 142.

Chapter 8: Christian Liberation and Transgendered People

1. Larry Gross, "Out of the Mainstream: Sexual Minorities and the Mass Media," in *Remote Control: Television, Audiences, and Cultural Power*, ed. Ellen Seiter et al. (New York: Routledge, 1989), 130–34.

2. Marcus J. Borg, *The God We Never Knew: Beyond Dogmatic Religion to a More Contemporary Faith* (San Francisco: HarperSan-Francisco, 1997), 100.

3. Rita Nakashima Brock, *Journeys by Heart: A Christology of Erotic Power* (New York: Crossroad, 1998), xi.

4. Gary David Comstock, "Aliens in the Promised Land? keynote address for the 1986 National Gathering of the United Church of Christ's Coalition for Lesbian/Gay Concerns," *Homosexuality and Religion,* ed. Richard Hasbany (New York: Harrington Park Press, 1979), 140.

5. Kwok Pui Lan, "God Weeps with Our Pain," in *New Eyes for Reading,* ed. John S. Pobee and Bärbel von Wartenberg-Potter (Geneva: World Council of Churches, 1996), 92.

6. Ibid., 90.

7. Heyward, *Saving Jesus from Those Who Are Right* (Minneapolis: Fortress Press, 1999), xiv.

8. Borg, *The God We Never Knew,* 99.

9. Gustavo Gutiérrez as quoted by James Bacik, *Contemporary Theologians* (Allen, Tex.: Thomas More/Tabor Publishing, 1989), 175.

10. For an intriguing view of this chapter in the life of Israel, see Robert Allen Warrior's provocative essay "A Native American Perspective: Canaanites, Cowboys, and Indians" (*Christianity and Crisis* 49, no. 12 [1989]). Warrior offers a challenging look at the Exodus story and draws out implications for biblical interpretation that are rarely considered.

11. Stephen Breck Reid, *Experience and Tradition* (Nashville: Abingdon Press, 1990), 69–70.

12. See James B. Nelson's powerful discussion of theological tradition in his book *Body Theology* (Louisville: Westminster/John Knox Press, 1992), 62–65. Nelson writes insightfully about the truth and significance that is to be found in taking our spiritual tradition seriously, as well as the importance of questioning that tradition when necessary.

13. Borg, *The God We Never Knew,* 100.

14. Eleazar Fernandez, *Toward a Theology of Struggle* (Maryknoll, N.Y.: Orbis, 1994), 172.

15. Renita J. Weems, "Reading Her Way through the Struggle: African American Women and the Bible," from *Stony The Road We Trod: African American Biblical Interpretation,* ed. C. Felder (Minneapolis: Fortress Press, 1991), 63.

16. Fernandez, *Toward a Theology of Struggle,* 172–73.

17. Carlos Mesters, "The Use of the Bible in Christian Communities of the Common People," from *The Challenge of Basic Christian Communities: Papers from the International Ecumenical Congress of Theology, São Paulo, Brazil* (Maryknoll, N.Y.: Orbis, 1980), 201.

18. Mesters, "The Use of the Bible in Christian Communities of the Common People," 202–3.

19. Ada María Isasi-Díaz, "The Bible and Mujerista Theology," from *Women of God, Women of the People* (St. Louis: Chalice Press, 1995), 261.

20. Isasi-Díaz, *Women of God, Women of the People*, 14–15.
21. Heyward, *Saving Jesus from Those Who Are Right*, 6.

Chapter 9: Elements of Emancipation for Transgendered Christians

1. Rik Isensee, *Reclaiming Your Life* (Los Angeles: Alyson Books, 1997), 6.
2. Ibid.
3. As I write these words I am viewing research indicating that at least fourteen differently gendered people were killed in the year 2000 due to anti-transgender violence. The year 2000 was not, unfortunately, atypical.
4. Sara Diamond, *Spiritual Warfare: The Politics of the Christian Right* (Boston: South End Press, 1989). Diamond documents right-wing religious efforts to oppose civil rights for gay, lesbian, bisexual, and transgendered people.
5. Rosemary Radford Ruether, *Sexism and God Talk* (Boston: Beacon Press, 1983), 24.
6. Carter Heyward, *Staying Power: Reflections on Gender, Justice, and Compassion* (Cleveland: Pilgrim Press, 1995), 69.
7. Ibid., 72, 76.
8. Heyward, *Staying Power*, 20.
9. Ada María Isasi-Díaz, "Introduction," *Women of God, Women of the People* (St. Louis: Chalice Press, 1995), 21.
10. Robert Nugent and Jeannine Gramick, "Homosexuality: Protestant, Catholic, and Jewish Issues; A Fishbone Tale," in *Homosexuality and Religion*, ed. Richard Hasbany (New York: Harrington Park Press, 1979), 31.
11. James B. Nelson, *Body Theology* (Louisville: Westminster/John Knox Press, 1992), 32.

Chapter 10: The Struggle for Inclusion

1. Gary David Comstock, "Aliens in the Promised Land? keynote address for the 1986 National Gathering of the United Church of Christ's Coalition for Lesbian/Gay Concerns," in *Homosexuality and Religion*, ed. Richard Hasbany (New York: Harrington Park Press, 1979), 139–40.
2. Parker J. Palmer, *The Courage to Teach* (San Francisco: Jossey-Bass, 1998), 37.
3. John Shelby Spong, *Here I Stand: My Struggle for a Christianity of Integrity, Love, and Equality* (San Francisco: HarperSanFrancisco, 2000), 134.
4. Peter J. Gomes, *The Good Book: Reading the Bible with Mind and Heart* (New York: Avon Books, 1996), 57.

5. See Robert Nugent and Jeannine Gramick, "Homosexuality: Protestant, Catholic, and Jewish Issues: A Fishbone Tale," *Homosexuality and Religion*, ed. Richard Hasbany (New York: Harrington Park Press, 1989), 30–31.

6. Palmer, *The Courage to Teach*, 38.

7. Ibid.

8. Ibid., 37.

9. Ibid., 38.

10. Carolyn Henninger Oehler, "Toward an Integrated Spirituality," in *Shaping Sanctuary: Proclaiming God's Grace in an Inclusive Church*, ed. Kelly Turney (Chicago: Reconciling Congregation Program, 2000), 5.

11. Barbara Anne Keely, *Faith of Our Foremothers: Women Changing Religious Education* (Louisville: Westminster/John Knox Press, 1997), 5–6.

12. Henninger Oehler, "Toward an Integrated Spirituality," 10.

13. Ibid.

14. Ada María Isasi-Díaz, *Women of God, Women of the People* (St. Louis: Chalice Press, 1995), 267.

Chapter 11: The Needs and Hopes of Transgendered Christians

1. Linda's name and the details of her letter have been changed to protect her anonymity.

2. Sidney G. Hall, "No Longer at Ease," *Shaping Sanctuary: Proclaiming God's Grace in an Inclusive Church*, ed. Kelly Turney (Chicago: Reconciling Congregation Program, 2000), 20.

3. Gerald P. Mallon, ed., "Preface: An Ecological Perspective of Social Work Practice with Transgendered Persons," *Social Services with Transgendered Youth* (New York: Harrington Park Press, 1999), xvii.

4. Wendell D. Glenn, "Reflections of an Emerging Male-to-Female Transgendered Consciousness," in *Social Services with Transgendered Youth*, ed. Gerald D. Mallon (New York: Harrington Park Press, 1999), 94.

5. Paraphrased and adapted from Richard Hasbany, preface, *Homosexuality and Religion* (New York: Harrington Park Press, 1989), 2.

6. Thomas Merton, *He Is Risen* (Niles, Ill.: Argus Communications, 1975), 16.

7. Patrick Gambill-Read, "Peniel, Pronouns, and Pookas," sermon given at a chapel service of United Theological Seminary of the Twin Cities, September 21, 2000, 9; used with permission.